TONY HART

TONY HART

A PORTRAIT
OF MY DAD

CAROLYN ROSS

JOHN BLAKE

Published by John Blake Publishing Ltd,
3 Bramber Court, 2 Bramber Road,
London W14 9PB, England

www.johnblakepublishing.co.uk

First published in hardback in 2010

ISBN: 978-1-84358-184-0

British Library Cataloguing-in-Publication Data:

A catalogue record for this book is available from the British Library.

Design by www.envydesign.co.uk

Printed in the UK by CPI William Clowes Beccles NR34 7TL

1 3 5 7 9 10 8 6 4 2

Papers used by John Blake Publishing are natural, recyclable products made from wood
grown in sustainable forests. The manufacturing processes conform to the
environmental regulations of the country of origin.

For Hattie and Ali
who loved my father too.

ACKNOWLEDGMENTS

With enormous thanks to Brian and Mary Davies; Michael Hart; Simon Hart; Fairy Gopsill; Yvonne Talbot; Rosemary Gill; Cliff Michelmore; Rooney Massara; Lady Judy Martin; Barry Chapman; Guglielmo del Pizzo; the Capraro family; Ray Alan; Neil Buchanan; Clive Doig; David Sproxton; Peter Lord; Christopher Pilkington; Chris Tandy; Sir Anthony Jay; Roc Renals; Colin Bennett; Simon and Penny Scott; Cliff White; Gabrielle Bradshaw; Lady Victoria Getty; Susie Ross; John Faulkener; Colonel William Shuttlewood; Maud Eager; Maree Aldred and Ruth Steadman for sharing their stories with me, for letting me reproduce their precious drawings and pictures, and for allowing me to use their fab photographs.

Also to Ed Wilson and John Wordsworth who turned the project into reality.

And to my darling man Ross for his love, support and encouragement – and for his sensible suggestions when my hyperbole became too great.

CONTENTS

FOREWORD

In the world of entertainment, so they say, you won't get far without good luck, good timing and good friends. Well it might be a cliché, but from my experience, it's simply the truth. I was lucky enough to come along at exactly the right moment in a golden age of children's television and I was more than lucky – blessed indeed – to work alongside one of the great performers of that time – my mentor, collaborator and big mate, Tony Hart.

We met at BBC TV Centre, sometime in the mid 70s. The producer of the highly successful children's programme *Vision On* had invited me in to discuss a new series that he was planning and to meet with its presenter – Tony. Of course I was totally in awe. He was already a famous TV personality, admired, loved and respected by viewers of all ages, whereas I – well, you couldn't really call me a *performer*, I was more of a... well, more of a ball of modelling clay actually. I was fresh from the packet and new to the business, not much more than a lump of terracotta Plasticine with a talent for changing shape. If I had ears, I'd have been wet behind them.

Several of us 'smaller performers' – as we like to call ourselves – had recently broken into television, following in the footsteps of Dougal and Zebedee. But it was a fiercely competitive world. The Clangers, with their radical chic politics and musical voices, were frankly intimidating. The Wombles were noisy, furry extroverts with compelling green credentials and a catchy theme tune. There scarcely seemed room for another newcomer, let alone one made of modelling clay.

But Tony must have seen something, some spark of talent beneath the fingerprints. He was generous enough, and big enough, to share his own show – *Take Hart*, no less – with a slightly gooey newcomer. He invited me in, partnered me, translated for me, fed me my lines, and every so often gently squished me up into a ball if I was getting above myself.

We hit it off immediately. Tony introduced himself with that infectious smile, and his customary quiet courtesy. Very much in awe, I blurted out my name and the usual rubbish that comes spilling out when you meet a famous person. Tony listened attentively, and nodded wisely. I couldn't believe it; he'd got every word. This was an absolute revelation to me; for years people had been staring blankly at me while I spoke, shrugging their shoulders, or giving me one of those watery smiles that says as clearly as can be 'I've no idea what you're talking about.' Not so with Tony. He had that precious knack of engagement with people. I often saw it in later years, whether he was talking to an autograph-hunting child or to a member of the *Take Hart* crew. He was always attentive and interested – a true listener – he had time for everyone and made all of us feel valued.

If I hadn't met him, on that memorable day at the TV Centre, my life would have been very different. It was Tony, and our long and happy partnership, that saved me from going the way of so much modelling clay – crammed into the Lego or trampled into the carpet. It's the simple truth: I owe my entire career to that most delightful of men.

I always looked up to Tony – I suppose I had no option really. As an artist, a performer, and a professional he was the perfect role model, but I saw all too little of him off-duty. Our worlds were just too far apart. Although he popped round a few times socially, he always found my box a little too cramped for comfort.

So it's a great joy now, through Carolyn's words, to hear not only about the public Tony that we all knew and loved, but also about Tony off-camera and in private: husband, father, artist, traveller and bon viveur. He enjoyed a wonderful full life with family and friends, in the spotlight and in private. It's a life in which I'm proud to have played a small, mischievous part.

Enjoy it!

Morph

(with a little help from Peter Lord CBE, the co-founder of Aardman Animations)

INTRODUCTION

I have often been asked how it makes me feel to have Tony Hart for a father. Proud, is my reply. Proud of his talent, proud of his fame, and so proud of the high esteem in which he is held not only by his family, friends and colleagues, but also by all those people who have watched him on television over the years, and who right up until his recent death were still stopping him in the street to say thank you.

When my mother died quite suddenly, I told my father that I would visit every week to see how he was, and to keep the accounts books up to date. Thinking that it would also be good for us both to have a project to keep us busy, I suggested that we put together his biography. 'What a good idea,' he said, 'and I know just how it should start!' But before we start with his words, let me add that this labour of love is as nothing compared to the love, advice, good sense and laughter that he has given me all through my life.

But enough of this sentiment. Let me give you Pa's own opening words:

The summer sun shone down out of a cloudless sky on to the golden sand and sparkling blue sea of a Kent coast beach. A tiny boy raced across the sand, tripped and fell flat on his face in a pool of sea water. Two strong hands gripped the sodden child under the armpits and lifted him up. 'Oh Tony boy,' said a deep and well-loved voice. 'What is your mother going to say?'

The tiny boy was my father, TV artist Tony Hart, known to pretty much everyone born between 1950 and 1990 who watched television. The two strong hands belonged to his father – my grandfather, Norman Chandler Hart, who gave my father a piece of advice when he was still a young boy. Disliking his office job in Maidstone but compelled to hold on to it in order to meet his financial commitments, he told my father: 'Never work in an office.' And he never did.

Although born Norman Antony Hart on 15 October 1925, my father went through his entire life being known not as Norman or Antony but as Tony, at school, in the army, and of course on television. Tony adored his father and spent his early childhood years with him, his mother Evelyn, and his younger brother Michael in a semi-detached house in Hastings Road, Maidstone in Kent, passing much of his time lying on the floor on his tummy drawing on the backs of envelopes. Norman was no mean artist himself, and many years later he and I would spend hours drawing together. He would carefully pencil a beautiful countryside scene – fields, trees, fences and birds – which I would completely ruin by adding a wobbly cow, or a thick-ankled horse with six legs. With Tony Hart for a father, I am happy to say that my drawing has improved since then.

BLANK CANVAS

On a plain sheet of white paper, Tony draws a few wiggly horizontal lines with a fine black marker pen. Then, with a thicker blue watercolour marker, he adds a few more straight lines, one above the other. Taking up the black marker again, he draws a similar shape to the one already there, but adds something else – a twig.

As he draws, he quietly talks to his audience about what he is doing while music plays in the background. He talks as if his audience members are his friends – and as if each and every one of them has an understanding of what he is showing them. Next, he fills in the two shapes with a few green lines, adding some yellow, which he drags through the green to brighten the colour. Lastly, he draws a wet brush through the blue lines to create a tranquil, watery scene in which two logs are floating.

But all is not quite as it seems. With the swift addition of the twig to one log, and a pair of nostrils to the other, a single log floats along a peaceful river accompanied by a crocodile.

A nine-year-old child is not an entirely blank canvas. By that age, many things have already happened to help form his character – the love of his family, trips to the seaside, nursery school and, in this instance, the first hesitant scribbles, which would later develop into a brilliant artistic talent.

We first bump into my father when he is nine years old because it was only then that things changed in what had so far been an idyllic life. His own father, Norman, had long established himself as a hero in his son's eyes ever since he had pulled Tony the toddler from a salty pool of water on a sun-drenched Kent beach into which he had tipped himself by running too fast across the wet sand. Tony's mother, Evelyn, all soft beauty and kindness, doted on him, and even the arrival of younger brother Michael when Tony was five merely added to the happy family life of the Harts in their pre-war Maidstone home.

A word about my father's drawing back then... Although the family was reasonably comfortable – indeed, Evelyn's side of the family was once described to me by my maternal grandmother as being no less than posh – reams of paper or drawing pads were not in evidence. So the young Tony drew on the backs of envelopes. And he drew mainly clocks – or tick-tocks as he called them – with a pencil, lying on the floor of the sitting room, listening to the rumble of the trolley buses as they sparked and rattled their way down Hastings Road into the town. He also drew at nursery school on the blackboards, on paper, with pencils and wax crayons and with chalk. He drew at meal times (*'Put the paper and pencils away now, darling, and eat your food.'*), in bed under the covers with the aid of a torch, in the kitchen, in the garden, everywhere, and, as he grew older, he stopped drawing clocks and began to draw everything else – people, toys, trees, buildings and animals.

So we find Tony, a happy nine-year-old, drawing patterns on the misty window of a steam train heading towards London in 1934 – and towards something ugly that was to appear on the joyous canvas that represented his young life so far.

Full of excitement, Tony was on his way to London to attend an audition for a place at the boy's choir school of All Saints in Margaret Street. Sam Randall, an uncle, had been a chorister at All Saints a generation before, and his son John had just been accepted there. Learning that his nephew also possessed a good singing voice, Sam had recommended All Saints to Tony's parents. Norman and Evelyn were enthusiastic about the idea and so he swiftly found himself, clean of face and shiny of shoe, travelling up to London in the care of one Mrs Drake, a Maidstone music teacher who, although very kind, would not permit him to lean out of the carriage window in case the flakes of ash and soot from the steam engine dirtied his face and clothes.

From Victoria Station, they crossed London by taxi and pulled up outside the Victorian brick church of All Saints, set amidst the iron railings and dusty pavements of the West End. They went inside and after a short wait in the hallway of the school building, Tony was summoned to a room where he sang his audition piece, Brahms's *Lullaby*, to the small audience of the principal and the choirmaster – and was politely, but instantly, rejected. Given the advice to 'train him up a bit more before we audition him again', Mrs Drake bustled the desperately disappointed Tony away. They walked together up Margaret Street and into the West End where, to cheer him up, she took him into a Lyons Corner House. Fancy cakes and wandering gypsy violinists went some way towards making up for his disillusionment, before they embarked on the return journey home to Maidstone.

It was only a few weeks later that All Saints contacted Mrs Drake again to tell her that puberty had struck, the voice of one of the older choristers had suddenly broken, and a vacancy had arisen – would she please bring him in to audition again? So Tony and Mrs Drake made the journey up to London once more, and this time, to his delight, he was accepted. In later life, I asked him what sort of a singing voice he had had as a boy. He said that he would never have been soloist material, although, he mused thoughtfully, to have got in at all must have meant he wasn't bad.

The euphoria of being accepted as a chorister quickly evaporated when at the start of his first term at All Saints, he found himself once again on the train bound for Victoria, but this time clutching his suitcase and choking back the tears. His father had already left for work, so Norman could not accompany Tony to the station and their goodbyes had already been said. But the railway line passed close by Norman's office building and, knowing exactly which train his boy was on, his father waved a tea towel out of his office window as it went by. It must have been a wonderfully heartening message for a young boy, knowing that everyone would see the distant flapping white signal but that it was a message of love and encouragement for him alone.

Life at All Saints was a strange existence, privileged in some ways – there were only 14 boys at the choir school, with normal lessons interwoven between choir practice and services. The classroom and dormitories were in a separate building from the church, reached across a small paved courtyard set behind iron gates leading off Margaret Street. Under the tutelage of their young choirmaster, one William Lloyd Webber – who in later life went on not only to compose *Serenade for Strings,* one of my father's favourite pieces of music, but also to father Andrew and Julian – the boys learned the hymns and harmonies and the rite and ritual of the Anglican church. They only came into contact with the adult members of the choir in the church, and my father remembers one of them miscounting the hallelujahs in the 'Hallelujah Chorus', and belting out at the top of his voice to the delight of the boys, 'Hallelujah! Hallelujah! Hallelujah! Halle – damn!'

Each morning, one chorister would have to get up an hour before the rest to go and serve as an altar boy amidst the gloom and incense at the early morning service. This did, however, bring its own privilege: Matron would specially cook the boy an egg, even asking how he wanted it done. Once the serving chorister had eaten his egg in solitary splendour and was safely despatched across to the church, Matron would run two cold baths in the bathroom on the floor below their dormitory, and then go and wake the other boys. On her shout of 'Next!' the boys would strip off their pyjamas and run naked in pairs down the stairs, leap into a bath, splash and leap out again. Seriously character-building stuff. After breakfast came lessons and these were taken at 14 desks squeezed into a small classroom lined with books. Everything seemed small at All Saints. The three youngest boys slept in a little room close to Matron, while the remaining 11 slept in a room not much bigger on the floor above. It should have been more fun than it actually was, but the consequences of any boy being caught out of bed or larking about during the night would not just mean a reprimand, but also a beating.

Behind the doors of All Saints the principal, Father Foster, ruled the choristers with a discipline that went beyond everything that we would deem politically correct, or just downright decent, today. There was a points system in operation. Any misdemeanours during the week, which included singing a wrong note in church, or making a blot or a spelling mistake in a workbook in class, would be totalled up on the Sunday; if they added up to a certain amount, the boys would be summoned in turn to the Father's study, where they would be chastised and beaten – sometimes with a wooden paddle, sometimes with a cane.

The beatings alone wouldn't have been so bad, and doubtless some were well earned. But once over, all the boys wanted to do was to get away as quickly as possible, to rub the tears of pain and humiliation out of their eyes. Having administered the beating, however, Father Foster would put away the cane and then stroke and kiss the boys' bottoms, while crooning soft words of contrition. It was monstrous behaviour, which neither my father, nor his brother later on – nor it seems any of the pupils – ever spoke of to their parents. The boys instinctively knew that behaviour of this nature was wrong; but it was being perpetrated by the man whose very position commanded obedience. The dichotomy this presented was impossible for them to understand.

The summons to the study for any wrongdoer was by means of an electric bell. Each boy had his own code, and my father's was two long rings, which meant that later, even when grown up, Tony could never quite hear an old-fashioned telephone ring without an inward flinch. But in spite of Father Foster's revolting little ways, the boys did manage to have some fun and found a good deal to laugh about.

One morning, at Easter, the choristers took their places in the choir stalls as usual and prepared to sing. Before they could draw breath, to their total amazement a group of men clad in long black robes with tall black hats and bearing long grey beards approached the chancel. There, in the dim light on the steps leading up to the altar, they proceeded to make a cake, wielding flour, milk and eggs with all due solemnity. For a chorister to laugh in church bore the penalty of a serious beating or even expulsion. Mere eye contact with another chorister was a corporal offence. But as we're all aware, when we are not supposed to laugh something mildly humorous becomes terribly funny, and my father and his fellow choristers – mischievous boys all aged between nine and thirteen – were stuffing handkerchiefs into their mouths, biting the insides of their cheeks and doubling over in a futile attempt not to laugh at the cake-making black-clad greybeards.

Needless to say, the cane was wielded with a vengeance after the cake-making episode. Had the boys been told that visiting Greek Orthodox priests were going to make a holy Easter cake in the church as part of their religious ceremony, it is possible they could have treated the occasion with the solemnity it deserved. Then again, they probably couldn't have.

The choristers sang twice a day and, of course, on Christmas Eve and Christmas Day, which meant that for Tony, living a long way away from the school, Christmas with his family did not really start until Boxing Day. Happily, there were compensations: tasty pork sausages for supper on Christmas Eve – a rare treat during wartime, and a visit to Drury Lane and the pantomime. And there was some comfort to be had in the ever-present shape of Matron who, whilst providing a kindly mother-figure for the younger boys, also ran the sanitarium with military precision.

At one point, Tony developed a large and interesting boil on his forearm. This was dressed and coated with unguents but continued to flourish. Matron surveyed the offending boil one morning and told the young Tony, 'We're going to have to lance it.' Pale with fright, Tony gasped, 'Oh no, Matron, please don't lance it!' 'Now then,' she said, 'be my brave ducky.' Thus exhorted, Tony bore up with fortitude and his boil was duly lanced with a cauterised darning needle, producing a very satisfactory eruption of pus, and rapidly healed.

For those seeking her ministrations, the route to Matron's room was along a narrow corridor, which was always referred to as 'Matron's Back Passage' accompanied by adolescent snickering. Rather fond of Matron, the young Tony always felt this was not quite the done thing.

Aside from dealing with minor ailments, singing and doing his lessons, Tony made the discovery that he was a reasonable actor, and took part in the school plays. His first role was two lines as Dunois's page in Bernard Shaw's *St Joan*. Waiting by the river, the page leaps to his feet crying, 'See, see, there she goes!' Dunois, who has been sitting gazing dreamily at the water replies, 'Who? The maid!' 'No,' replies the page, 'the kingfisher!' Tony poured his heart and soul into his tiny role while the part of Joan was, he says, brilliantly played by one of the other boys.

The roles he acted in subsequent school productions grew larger until he was eventually cast in the leading role of Francis of Assisi in *The Little Plays of Saint Francis*. Among the audience at one of these performances was Shayle Gardner, an American actor not entirely without influence in the film industry. He was so impressed by Tony's performance that he wanted to take him to the States to pursue an acting career, and suggested this to Norman and Evelyn who, unsurprisingly, were not in favour of the idea.

In a letter penned many years later to Brian Davies, a fellow-pupil who played St Francis's sidekick Brother Juniper in *The Little Plays of St Francis*, my father describes Shayle Gardner as looking like Toulouse Lautrec's painting of Aristide Bruant – complete with black hat, scarf and cape. It seems Mr Gardner would not have been entirely appropriate as a guide and mentor to the young Tony, as he nonplussed the boys at All Saints by insisting that they all visit a London gallery to admire a nude sculpture. The insidious Father Foster also persuaded Tony's parents that the American was 'not suitable' for a boy of my father's age to travel with – a view shared by Brian Davies, who recalls Shayle Gardner as being a very strange man. This may have been the case, but it is interesting to reflect for a moment on what might have happened if he had gone. In his letter to Brian, Tony reflects that Gardner must have had visions of another Freddie Bartholomew – a British child actor who became popular in the 1930s in such Hollywood films as *Anna Karenina* and *Little Lord Fauntleroy*.

But a career in Hollywood was not to be, and Tony stayed on at school where, in the summer months, he and the other boys would be taken out into the countryside for walks and, at the end of term, play cricket matches – pupils against fathers. Tony's father Norman, bowling against the younger boys, took it gently. One of the other fathers – the father of Saint Joan, in fact – went all out and bowled hard, fast and furious balls at the boys. Going out to bat, one of these hit Tony square in the teeth, and for decades afterwards he smiled with the lopsided smile he had developed to hide the broken front tooth. It was decades later, when he was in his sixties, that he finally had the tooth crowned and was able to smile with a broad toothy grin – but only when he remembered. The lopsided smile is the natural one.

My father was one of the 'Saturday Boys'. Any chorister who lived near enough to go home on a Saturday did so, but had to be back by four o'clock in the afternoon to prepare for Evensong. Maidstone was much too far for Tony to go home for the day, so he and the other Saturday Boys would go walking in Regents Park, or wander into the West End to gaze covetously over the delights to be found in the windows of Woolworths or Hamleys toy shop.

The school holidays of course were spent blissfully at home in

Maidstone in the company of Tony's parents, his brother Michael, and Peggy, their terrier. But a dark shadow was cast as the summer holidays of 1939 drew to a close when the family, gathered around the radio, heard Prime Minister Neville Chamberlain announce that Britain had declared war on Germany. A subdued hush descended upon the Harts, a mood that remained unbroken until my father, who had run upstairs, came running back down clutching his air rifle and saying, 'Don't worry – I'll protect you!'

The remainder of Tony's schooling took place during the war years. With 1940 came the first bombings over London, and the boys of All Saints were evacuated to a large country house in Sussex. There they were reasonably safe, although there were some air raids. The boys were alerted to the first one by what sounded to them like a faint knocking sound, but which was actually the distant crump of bombs exploding. Father Foster came flying downstairs in a panic calling to the boys to go down to the cellars where they stayed in safety until the sounds ceased. It didn't take long for Tony to discover that by knocking softly on the wood panelling in the classroom during a tedious lesson he could produce a very similar sound to the distant bombs, and Father Foster, turning pale, would leap to his feet and order the boys to the safety of the cellar.

Back at home, the Hart family had been issued with a Morrison shelter – a steel indoor shelter with meshed sides that was over six feet long and four feet wide and designed to shield the family in the event of a bomb falling on their house. It also served my father as a brilliant studio table for his artwork when, during the holidays, he would draw to order for Michael and his friends.

In 1940 the years at All Saints finally came to an end, and the 15-year-old Tony won a scholarship to Clayesmore, a boys' public school in Dorset. He and his mother Evelyn went on the train to look at the school set deep in the heart of the countryside. They were shown the dormitories, the classrooms, the chapel, the grounds, and when my father said he was interested in painting and drawing, the art studio. This, he thought, was heaven!

Life at Clayesmore was to contrast sharply with the strictures of All Saints. There were no cold baths and no beatings. There were punishments certainly, but a typical one would be three 'rollers'. This meant the boys had to run up and down the cricket pitch three times with the heavy roller that flattened the ground – it was more like fun than a punishment, and it served a useful purpose. These were happy years for him. He admits to doing well in Art and English but was pretty bad at everything else.

As a child, I loved to hear stories from his schooldays, particularly any that had anything to do with his friend Gibson. Gibson was in the same year as my father and famous for doing anything that was silly, annoying or just funny. Once, during a game of rugby, the ball was thrown into a tree where it stuck fast. 'Gibson, get up that tree and get the ball down,' instructed the sports master. Gibson obligingly scrambled up into the branches of the tree, retrieved the ball and sat there, hugging it to his chest. 'Well, come on, boy, throw it down!' barked the sports master. Gibson cuddled the ball tighter to his chest. 'No!' he replied with a happy smile. 'Gibson, I'm warning you, throw that ball down now!' 'No!' came the reply once more. 'Gibson, if you don't pass that ball down right now…' Grinning knowingly at each other, Tony and the rest of the boys abandoned the game, knowing that if Gibson had decided to stay in his tree with the ball, it was going to be a long time before he came down.

Apart from rationing, the cold fingers of war did not penetrate too deeply into the Dorset countryside. At home in Maidstone during the holidays it was quite a different matter – with Norman and Evelyn even telling my father not to come home straight away at the end of one term, as his journey would take him through

London and the bombing raids. Ever the obedient son, my father completely ignored this advice and got home perfectly safely, much to his parents' annoyance and delight. One day sitting out in the garden, Tony heard the sound of some kind of aircraft, but not like any he had heard before. Looking up, he saw a sinister looking object flying high overhead – it was the first of the V1s, or Doodlebugs, as they were known – an unmanned flying bomb on its way to London. Quickly, my father made a sketch of the wicked looking rocket-shaped object with its boxy wings and tail, and took it to the local Maidstone newspaper where it appeared in the next issue. These Doodlebugs were fuelled with petrol and set on a course to London over Kent. When the petrol was used up, the engine would cut out and the bomb would fall to earth. People in the capital city (including my mother who was a child in Paddington at the time) would hear the engine stop, and would know it would be ten seconds before the bomb hit the ground and exploded. After my father's drawing of the first one appeared in the paper, Doodlebugs became a common sight as they droned high in the sky over the eastern counties on their deadly mission towards London.

Back in the leafy, peaceful countryside of Dorset, Tony was discovering there were many more things to do at Clayesmore than there had been at All Saints – which had really only offered reading, writing, arithmetic and choral singing. Clayesmore offered a wealth of subjects and activities. Almost as soon as Tony arrived, he volunteered to join the Army Cadets. He quickly discovered that he liked maps and map reading, and became very good at it. He was also a good marksman with a rifle and won several competitions. And once again, he took part in the school plays, making a perfectly acceptable young lady as Cecily in *The Importance of Being Earnest.*

And it was at Clayesmore that my father's talent for drawing was first noted and nurtured – at All Saints they hadn't been interested.

His art master was the first real artistic influence in Tony's life, teaching him everything he could about the subject and providing encouragement, although little was needed. It was this master, the waspish but witty Mr Scadding, who recognised that the young Tony was concentrating solely on linear drawing. He told my father that he was missing out on a lot and immediately undertook to introduce him to other mediums – showing him how to lay colour and which brushes to use, and putting him right in his painting when things went wrong. For my father, this tutelage in his favourite subject, combined with the beauty and grandeur of Clayesmore, was indeed heaven.

It seems the sharpest memories of youth tend to be drawn from the summer months, and when combined with love and music, the nostalgic sweetness of the memory is almost tangible. Such is an image of Clayesmore that my father treasured. It was summer, and some of the boys were rehearsing *The Yeomen of the Guard* by Gilbert & Sullivan on the lawn. The rest of the boys were lying around on the grass in the sunshine watching and listening to the music, and sitting up among them, dressed all in white, was the trim and youthful shape of the Assistant Matron with whom, unbeknownst to her, my father was hopelessly in love.

I visited both of my father's schools. Clayesmore gives an impression of quiet grandeur, its stately brick buildings glowing peacefully in the sunshine, its extensive grounds, brushed with green lawns and shaded by majestic trees, breathe peace and tranquillity. It is worlds removed from All Saints. Peeking through the church doors, my impression was of a dim interior where feeble shafts of sunlight were waging an eternal war against the gloom, permeated by a subtle all-pervading smell evocative of age and decay. Not, perhaps, the ideal place for young boys to grow and develop – and especially not under the rule of Father Foster.

However, all experiences, both good and bad, help to form the character of a person, and, like the greatest masterpiece, it is necessary to have a mixture of light and shade in order to show the subject to its best advantage.

Despite the unhappy aspects of All Saints, my father left it with an enduring love for choral music, and some liking for high-church rite and ritual. The school eventually closed in 1968, and my father never went back to visit, although he met Father Foster once more, long after he had left All Saints. He had been drawing for children in Sidcup to raise money for their school and, knowing that this was where Father Foster now lived, he looked up his address in the phone book and went to his house. As he hesitated at the gate, the front door opened to reveal Father Foster's sister standing there smiling at him. 'We saw in the paper you would be here,' she said, 'and wondered if you would come.' Tony went in and was taken up to Father Foster's room. Now elderly and unwell, the man was in his pyjamas, sitting up in a chair by the bed. They talked pleasantly for a while about my father's work, and touched briefly on the things that had been fun at All Saints, but when Tony stood up to leave and held out his hand, Father Foster recoiled. 'Don't touch me!' he said. Trying to forget all that was repellent about the man, my father swiftly left the house.

He returned to Clayesmore, however, several times, and many years later on one such visit he encountered one of his former masters, now quite elderly, on the lawn where afternoon tea was in progress. 'Hello Sir!' he said. The old man peered at him. 'Ah, Hart N A isn't it?' My father agreed that it was. 'How is Hart M C?' Younger brother Michael was at the time appearing as an actor on stage in the West End. 'He's in *The Pyjama Game*, Sir,' replied Tony enthusiastically. The old man looked pensive. 'Hmm well, oh dear, is he? Still, I suppose somebody has to make them.'

A PASSAGE TO INDIA

Standing up in front of a live audience, Tony pins a large white sheet of paper to his easel. 'Tell me when you know what this is!' he says with a smile. In the centre of the paper with a fine black marker pen, he draws a martini glass, then two circles resembling black olives above it. 'Any idea?' he asks. 'Triangle! Wineglass! Spaceship!' His audience, enthusiastic but inaccurate, shout their suggestions.

'Let's see if this helps you.' Tony adds a blob of black to the base of the martini glass along with a couple of curved lines, then two more curves to the 'olives' above it, and then several straight lines, three or four each side of the stem of the glass. 'Now can you see what it is?' he asks. 'A face!' yells one youngster. 'You've got it!' says Tony with a grin, 'But the face of what?' 'Cat! Mouse! Picasso! Hamster!' The audience roars their ideas, multitudinous and colourful.

Tony selects a broad marker pen that is beginning to run out of ink. 'I like this one,' he tells his audience, 'because it gives you a soft, smudgy line.' He begins to add soft, broad lines radiating out from the martini glass, then more below it. The audience watches with breathless anticipation as he adds more lines until a voice shouts out 'Tiger!' And so it is.

With a war going on, and his schooldays behind him, there was never any question about my father joining one of the forces. His father had served in the army during World War I and was keen for Tony to follow him. But, at 18 years old, beguiled by the glamour of the Royal Air Force and determined to join in the war as a rear gunner, Tony made his way to London to attend an interview and medical for the RAF.

The interview went fine and my father endured the minor indignities of a thorough physical examination, with the last two tests being for hearing and eyesight. While sitting in the Medical Officer's sterile office, the doctor peered into my father's ears and then asked him to repeat what he said: 'Wild horses,' he muttered, almost inaudibly. 'Wild horses,' repeated my father. 'Peppermint,' he barely whispered. 'Peppermint.' repeated my father. Then Tony strained to hear the next words. 'Father Christmas!' he said. The doctor looked at him in amazement. 'But I haven't said it yet!' he exclaimed. With what seemed to be extra-sensory hearing, Tony submitted to the last test of all, on his eyesight – and failed. One eye was not up to scratch. 'I'm sorry,' he was told, 'but we cannot pass you for flight.' There were, they told him, plenty of desk jobs in the RAF where they were sure he would do very well, but for my father it was aircrew or nothing. Fighting back tears, he left the building and groped his way to a telephone box to call his father. 'Thank God!' exclaimed Norman when he heard the news. 'Let me get on to Brigadier Ponting straight away, and get you sorted you out with the Indian Army.'

When World War I had broken out in 1914, Tony's father had immediately volunteered for service, and was enrolled in the Royal West Kents as a PE instructor. All too soon most of his compatriots were sent to France, but the authorities would not let Norman go with them. 'We need you here,' he was told, 'to train up the new recruits and get them fit for combat.' Although he was longing to join in the war, good fortune was watching over Norman by keeping him in England, for hardly any of his fellows came back from the trenches of northern France. Eventually, the Royal West Kents let Norman go to India where he found himself training Gurkhas, the tough, courageous soldiers from Nepal. He liked them, and he liked India. The remaining war years saw him in action on the North-West Frontier and he stayed on afterwards, eventually returning home to Maidstone in 1921. As a boy of about six, my father liked nothing more on a Sunday morning than to fling himself into his parents' big bed and say, 'Tell me about India, Daddy.'

It was obvious that with the RAF ruled out, the next best thing for Tony was the Indian Army. Their recruiting base was in Maidstone, Tony's home town, so he spent some eight months in training at home before, aged 20, setting sail for India in 1945 on one of the big passenger liners commandeered by the forces. The young men at the training base came from all different backgrounds, and my father remembers some of them laughing at him and calling him a toff because he wore pyjamas to bed – he also remembers some of them sobbing into their pillows at night and calling for their mothers. My father, of course, had come to terms with homesickness at a much younger age.

Tony came through the training pretty much unscathed, although one of his friends had a very difficult time. This particular officer cadet always seemed to fall foul of the Regimental Sergeant Major. No matter what he did, there was always something at fault – his belt or boots weren't highly polished enough, his hat was on at the wrong angle – there was always something. This young man had acquired a very old regimental cap, and on the cap badge, which depicted a lamb carrying a flag, all the detail of the lamb's fleece had been worn completely smooth. By giving it a good polish, the badge stood out, shining like a star. One morning, determined to get everything perfect to impress his RSM, the cadet had been meticulous in his appearance – and the gleaming cap badge was the jewel in his personal crown. He stood in line with the others while the RSM strode slowly past the men, paused and then returned to stand in front of the young cadet. He looked him up and down and up again where his eyes came to rest on the smooth, gleaming cap badge. He took a step forwards, bringing his face within inches of the unfortunate cadet. 'Mr Smith, Sah!' he blared, 'have you ever seen a lamb with no fleece?' Unable to bear it, the young cadet replied half laughing, half crying, 'No Sergeant Major, but have you ever seen a lamb carrying a flag?'

The voyage to India was uneventful. The sleeping quarters in the cargo hold were hardly luxurious, but each man had a hammock, which proved to be perfectly comfortable. The ship finally docked at Bombay, and my father's first year was spent at the Indian Military Academy at Dehra Dun in the foothills of the Himalayas. A letter to his parents dated 26 November 1945 paints a vivid and entertaining picture of those last days of the Raj just before Partition. He writes mainly about three characters – his great friend and an officer cadet like himself, an Indian called Sat (pronounced Sart), Sat's father, Colonel Marya, and Mac – another British officer cadet. Due a short leave, he and Mac had gone to spend it with Sat at his home in Patiala in the Punjab, and he wrote the following about his first impressions:

'If only I'd been able to get a film. I can't describe the beautiful buildings they have there, Patiala is a very clean place and the buildings in the Gardens and in the Mall (where we lived) are of lovely eastern architecture and white, and in some cases salmon pink. In the sunlight they look pretty good – then there is the sacred pool and the Sikh Temple, all lovely, and very different from a place like DD [Dehra Dun], which is full of Europeans. In Patiala we didn't see a white man or woman for the whole time we were there.'

On their first evening in Patiala, they went out on the town.

'That evening, Col Marya took Mac and I to the Club where we were introduced to many of the "high-ups" including a Prince, he was a Rajah, and one of the present Maharajah's step-brothers, he was a Sikh and very pleasant. He told us about the old Maharajah who was evidently a bit of a lad, had 365 wives, and a few hundred cars – Daimlers. We saw the cars – they had been given to the State as taxis. We didn't see the wives. Just as well, they'd probably be a bit long in the tooth by now. Mac, quite innocently, asked "why 365 wives?" whereupon we all coughed like blazes and discussed the lovely climate.'

Although the letter is over 60 years old, it could have been written by anyone travelling today – remarking on the areas where the tourists hadn't yet penetrated, and with the rather coy reference to the Maharajah's sexual proclivities dressed down for the benefit of the parents.

Tony was surprised and delighted by the obvious affection Sat's family had for each other. When they first arrived at Sat's family home, Colonel Marya came out to greet them, and Sat made the traditional formal greeting to his father. In his letter, Tony writes: *'When Sat saw his father, he went on his knees and kissed his feet, this sounds rather funny of course but it was rather lovely really. They have these customs and stick to them very strictly.'* Sat's mother and sisters stayed behind a beaded curtain, and Sat went to them after greeting his father and was kissed and embraced by them all, but out of sight of their guests.

That first night, there was a large gathering for the evening meal to celebrate Sat's return home, and Tony hugely enjoyed all the curry, dhal and rice that was offered to him. The company, which was of course all male, sat cross-legged in a large circle on the floor helping themselves from the fragrantly spiced dishes that were placed in the centre, eating from their plates with their fingers and using chapatis to wipe up the delicious sauces. At the end of the meal, each man belched loudly in turn, signifying his approval of the feast. Perfectly capable of belching to order (a skill I must confess to having inherited), my father waited for his turn, and after the man seated beside him had belched, Tony produced a long and spectacular burp. The assembled company looked at him appalled. Tony looked askance at Sat who was trying not to laugh. 'It is correct for us to do this thing,' he explained, 'but very bad manners for you!'

Tony found, like his father, that he very much liked India and its people and their ways, and got on well with both his fellow British officers and his Indian counterparts who numbered both Sikhs and Hindus. He was both interested in and respectful of the different religions of his Indian friends. He particularly liked the Sikhs who were proud and warlike, and, when he shared a hut with one, he watched the ritual cleansing of the long hair and the binding of it into its turban with fascination.

At this time, the war in Europe had just ended, but there was much religious unrest in India. India had been the jewel in the crown of the British Empire for some considerable time but was now demanding her independence – further adding to the unrest. Very quickly my father became a junior officer, and was put through rigorous training which, he told me, included climbing a rope using only his arms with both legs held out straight in front of him and a full pack on his back. (I tried this myself in the gym at school without a pack on my back – hopeless!) He was 20 years old, and soon became very fit.

To go with his own newly acquired physique, Tony thought a narrow moustache would add a dashing touch. For some days he refrained from shaving his upper lip, and eventually some downy ginger fluff began to appear. One morning out on the parade ground, the Sergeant Major strutted past the line of young officers, swagger stick tucked under his arm. He passed Tony, stopped, turned round and came back. He peered into my father's face, walked slowly all round him, and came back to the front. 'Mr Hart, Sah!' he roared. Standing to attention, Tony stared straight ahead, wondering what was coming. 'Ruddy marigold, Sah!' bellowed the Sergeant Major, and strutted on down the line. At the next available opportunity, the fledgling moustache came off.

Once a month, there was a ritual in which my father, who was by then a captain, as the most senior British officer on duty always took part. Set slightly apart from the main camp within the compound, there was a wooden hut set at the top of a flight of steps. In this hut was a large cauldron, the contents of which were lovingly tended by one of the native Indians. On the appropriate day, my father would be roused by the Company Subedar-Major – the Indian military equivalent of a British RSM – and told, 'It is time, Sahib, you must be coming now.' Tony would put down the book he had been reading, and follow him out into the compound.

As they walked towards the hut, other Indian soldiers would appear in shorts and singlets, holding bits of cloth or sticks and grinning. 'Very well,' my father would say, 'but are all these people necessary?' 'They may be useful, Sahib,' would come the reply, and they would walk up the steps into the hut followed by everyone else. The cauldron was full of rakshi – a local home-brewed spirit that, if consumed in its raw state, would undoubtedly render a man blind and insane within moments. The dilution of the brew and its tasting was a ritual which had to be followed.

As the senior officer present, my father would be given the first taste in an old tin mug – which would have been brought by one of the soldiers. The mug would be wiped with a bit of cloth that had been brought by another, and then the contents of the cauldron would need to be stirred with a stick – which had been brought by yet another soldier. Tony would be given a brimming mug of the rakshi, which he had to empty and pronounce it good, and then invite the Subedar-Major to try it too. But of course, the Subedar-Major could not drink alone, so Tony would have to have another slug of the stuff. In strict order of rank, everyone would have to drink some; next, the man who had been tending the brew all month would have to try it – but of course not alone, and so the Subedar-Major would have to join him and so would my father. Then the soldier who had bought the mug would have to taste it – and so would the brewer, and so would the Subedar-Major and so would my father. Then the soldier who bought the cloth would have to taste it as well – and so would the soldier who bought the mug, the brewer, the Subedar-Major, and my father, now on his fifth mug. Finally, the soldier who had bought the stick would also have to try it – and so would the man who brought the cloth, and the man who brought the mug, and the brewer, and the Subedar-Major, and of course my father. The ritual complete to the satisfaction of everyone involved, my father would then attempt to walk smartly down the steps and back to his own hut – which he never achieved with the dignity he would have liked.

My father enjoyed alcohol, there is no doubt, and although not an excessive drinker, he did go over the top from time to time. In his letter recounting his trip to Sat's home in Patiala, he writes:

'I went on two shooting expeditions, I only got pigeon, partridge and plover, but we were after black buck and sambar, a type of deer. We used an old battered car with a high power Rolls-Royce engine, and chased these deer all over the Punjab! It was on the second of these shoots that I made my one mistake on leave. Coming back at 6pm, it got a bit chilly and old Gurbaix Singh passed around the whisky! Need I say more? The trouble was, I'd been invited to a wedding feast that night and when I did get there, I wasn't quite myself. Mac was very good and saw that I behaved, but I felt awful, I knew jolly well I was tight, so I tried to be very natural but that made it worse. Mac said I was talking much too carefully, it must have been most amusing. I vaguely remember having to take my shoes off and sit cross-legged on the floor – a socking great leaf was put in front of me and weird and wonderful concoctions dolloped into it.'

The first few months in India in the Indian Military Academy at Dehra Dun passed swiftly and peacefully, with one notable exception: my father and a number of officer cadets encountered a group of people in the town whose less than friendly attitude baffled them completely. Having been used to being acknowledged in a sociable way by the Indians as they made their way through the streets, the cadets could not understand why these people were spitting at them and shouting insults. It was only when the insults escalated to pushing and shoving and a scuffle was on the verge of breaking out that Tony realised that they had been mistaken for the

INA – the Indian National Army, a guerilla operation whose main aim was to overthrow the British in colonial India. Pointing frantically to the initials 'IMA' on his uniform, Tony managed to communicate his identity to the potential troublemakers, and peace was thankfully restored with much grinning and hand-shaking.

Once he'd completed his training in the IMA, Tony joined the 1st Gurkha Rifles, a regiment whose toughness had long distinguished itself as a fighting force. The British had first encountered the Nepalese Gurkhas more than a century before when they were fighting against them. So impressed were they with their fighting prowess that the British began to recruit the Gurkhas as mercenaries, eventually forming dedicated Gurkha regiments within the British Indian Army.

As part of his uniform, each 1st Gurkha Rifles officer was issued with a *kukri*, a curved knife, which came in its own special case together with two little skinning knives. Tony was taught how to draw the kukri from its case, whirling it high in the air around his wrist, before bringing it up short against the throat of his enemy. The purpose of the whirling, flashing blade was to confuse his opponent so that he could not tell which angle it was coming from, and was therefore impossible to block. To the end of his days, my father's kukri hung on the wall by the inglenook fireplace of his home, and many were the times the blade whistled past my neck as he demonstrated to interested visitors how the knife was drawn.

Only once did he have to use his kukri in earnest – not, I hasten to add, against another human being. He had been invited to a feast, and was given the dubious privilege of beheading the goat that was to be the main course. It was considered a great honour and it would have been terrible to refuse; and although he knew the theory of how this should be done, Tony was terrified of making a botch of it. The base of the blade of the kukri is thick and heavy, and it tapers to a razor-sharp edge. At the appointed time, my father presented himself, kukri in hand, to meet the goat. The animal's head was pulled forwards, and Tony took a firm stance, feet apart, and raised the kukri high. He swept it down with enough force that the thick base of the blade smashed through the top of the spinal column, then drew the blade through so that the sharp edge swept through the stringy tendons and flesh of the neck. It was neatly done, and my father hopes the animal didn't know too much about it. The curried goat served later at the feast was, he said, superb.

For the most part, Tony's time in India was hugely enjoyable. He had visions of pursuing a career in the military, becoming a crusty old colonel sporting a watery eye and a legendary moustache. He went hunting and spent a night up a tree with a gun watching for a panther that had been killing the local livestock. He kept a monkey as a pet, and got himself a job as a reporter for the military newsletter, which meant he was invited to every party, dance or ball going. He remembered how, at a formal ball, the women would wear white while the men provided the colour with their dress uniforms.

He was soon drafted into the concert party, appearing in plays put on to entertain the men. His Commanding Officer's wife also took part in these amateur dramatics, and he found himself on one occasion playing a scene where his character was required to kiss her. She was a naughty girl who took full advantage of the scene and could have led him astray, but he held his CO in high regard and did not, so to speak, rise to the challenge. His CO, I might add, eventually divorced his flighty wife.

But Tony's time in India was not all fun and games. It was 1947, and Partition was looming. There was unrest between the different faiths all over the country, particularly in the Punjab, which was populated mainly by Sikhs. My father's unit was called into Nagpur – which translates from Urdu as 'snake town' – to quell a riot. This in itself was not unusual, as the unit was often called out for this purpose, but generally they would reach the trouble spot to find the riot had already melted away. On this occasion, however, it had not. The unit of 1st Gurkha Rifles arrived on the scene, with Captain Hart in tow, aged all of 22, to find a large and angry crowd shouting and hurling missiles. In the dry, shimmering heat, the chief ringleader could be seen moving around in the background, encouraging the others to more violence, but keeping himself behind the women and children.

The CO was quick to assess the state of affairs, and knew the best way to defuse the situation causing the least injury or loss of life was to remove the ringleader – immediately and permanently. He called my father across, and asked him if he had a marksman in his unit. Although Tony was an excellent shot himself, there was another, better marksman among his men. He carried the orders from the CO to his marksman, telling him that if he could get a clear shot at the ringleader, to take him out. Cool as a cucumber, the marksman took aim with his rifle, waited until he was sure of his target, and fired. The man dropped dead instantly. For a moment all was confusion, then, with no one to direct the rioters, the crowd rapidly thinned. The remaining few who might have shown a last surge of defiance, when faced with the Gurkha unit ranked up, rifles cocked and aimed, quickly dissolved like smoke. But although my father had not fired the shot himself, by carrying the verbal order from the CO to his marksman, he felt a real responsibility for the loss of this unknown man's life.

Back in the mess, Tony, who was in some state of shock, was encouraged to have a drink, a natural reaction and a very good idea. Port was the drink in question, and the officers drank a great deal of it – and on this occasion saw to it that Tony drank even more. The result was that in due course my father was carried to his sleeping quarters, a hut with a small veranda, deposited outside his door and left to sleep it off. The next morning, he awoke on his veranda accompanied by a headache to end all headaches and a pile of vomit which had dried out in the morning sun – the first of only two experiences in his life where a few hours of his existence were completely lost to him through alcohol. The second was not to occur until some years later when he was out of the army and had embarked on his career as a television artist.

My father was generally pretty healthy, but whenever he did become ill it was never with anything trivial. As a young child of about ten, he contracted rheumatic fever, which confined him to his bed, flat on his back for six weeks. It was summertime, and a mirror was placed on the wall in his bedroom to reflect the garden through the window so he could watch his younger brother playing outside. Later in India, he withstood dysentery, which attacked some of his comrades, but succumbed to malaria. He remembers standing to attention in immaculate uniform, on parade, out in the blazing sun and feeling pretty crummy. It seemed to him that a blackness was closing in all round the periphery of his vision. Fascinated, he watched the blackness increase until all that was left to him was a tiny circle of vision, like looking down a gun barrel. Finally, that too disappeared, and, straight as a ramrod, he fell forwards flat on his face.

He woke up in the local hospital, and dimly remembers wanting an apple, and being most unreasonable about it. His CO came to visit him, and found himself confronted by an almost hysterical Captain Hart who was crying deliriously, 'But all I want is an apple!' Aware that the young officer was not quite himself, the CO patted my father soothingly on the shoulder and said, 'Look here old boy, we can't get you any apples, and you're upsetting the rest of the ward. Just be a good chap and shut up and eat what they give you. You'll soon be better.'

Sure enough, Tony was soon back on his feet, but a few years later, back home in England, he went to donate some blood. He had been hooked up to his tube with the needle, and the blood was dripping nicely into a bag while a doctor was off-handedly asking him if he'd ever had typhoid – no. Yellow fever? No. Malaria? Yes. 'Can't use this then,' said the doctor and pulled out the needle from Tony's arm. They didn't pour my father's blood down the sink; instead it went on to the rose bed outside.

Shortly before he left India for what was to be the last time, Tony got into trouble. After spending some time at the bar in the mess, he and some other young officers wheedled a Norton motorcycle out of supplies one Friday night, promising to return it first thing on the Monday. They then took it into the town and, in the main street, decided to see how many people they could get on it. At the first attempt, my father couldn't control the bike and they all fell off, so they tried again. My father would have like to say that there were nine people on the bike but thinks it was probably seven. Roaring with laughter and shouting encouragement to each other, the fledgling 1st Gurkha Rifles motorcycle display team wobbled its way down the main street. Of course the incident was reported to the Commanding Officer, and my father was given a serious dressing down and his long leave home cancelled. It seems severe for what appeared to be nothing more than a high-spirited prank, but the mood in India at that time was volatile and anti-British – English officers needed to be seen as the epitome of dignity and self-control.

By this time, Tony had acquired a girlfriend, Pamela, who was Anglo-Indian and very beautiful. Her grandmother was Indian and her English father ran the ice plant in Madras. The motorcycle incident having left him feeling humiliated and rather foolish, Tony avoided the Officers' Mess, and spent most of his free time with Pamela. One evening three weeks later, when he did venture into the Mess, he ran into one of his friends who clapped him on the back and congratulated him. 'What for?' asked Tony in bewilderment. 'Look at the board!' he was told. So he dutifully went to look at the board, which listed the names of those officers who had been selected to go home on long leave – and saw his name on the list. Then he saw the date he was due to go – it was the very next day! He tore into the town to say a heartbreaking goodbye to Pamela, and the next morning he grabbed his friend, and the two of them raced around to gather his kit together and get all the necessary paperwork signed. All went swimmingly with every senior officer available to sign off the appropriate forms until they went to get a signature from the Medical Officer pronouncing him fit to travel. He was not there, and Tony needed to be on his way. Nothing daunted, his friend signed the medical form for him.

Tony then travelled some 200 miles by train to Deolali, a large transit camp where soldiers travelling back to England were assembled, and the last port of call before heading off to Bombay. The CO at Deolali checked through the papers and when he got to the medical form, he raised an eyebrow and showed him the signature. Tony looked at it and his heart sank – his friend had signed the name 'D. Duck'. Regarding him frigidly, the CO told him to go all the way back and get all the documentation done again. Gloomily, Tony travelled back on the train, and had to sit it out for a week while he waited for the paperwork to be signed. Bored to tears, he visited the local cinema every evening to see the same film – *Blithe Spirit*. It was a good film but, after seven consecutive viewings, not one he ever felt the urge to see again.

Having already said his goodbyes to Pamela, my father had not let his girlfriend know that he was back in town, thinking it would be too painful. On his last day, however, one of his friends had let her know that he was back. Tony had already boarded the train standing at the station ready to head back to Deolali, and was leaning out of the window talking to another officer. The train slowly started to move. Just as it began to pull out of the station, my father glanced back down the train to find himself looking straight at Pamela who had just come on to the platform. She ran down the length of the train and, running alongside, she reached up to take his hand. All too quickly the train gathered speed, forcing her to release her hold. Gazing at each other as the train pulled away, he watched her figure recede into the distance, unaware that he would never see her again.

From Bombay, he spent five weeks sailing to Liverpool on a banana boat, the *Ascanious*, travelling with another 1st Gurkha Rifles officer known to all as 'Fairy' Gopsill. As always seems to be the case with anyone who has a nickname like Lofty or Tiny, there was no one broader, taller or more masculine than Fairy. Fairy was travelling back to England bound for Buckingham Palace where he was due to receive a medal for bravery. I asked my father what he had done. 'He never said,' he told me. I later found out that Fairy had been awarded the Military Cross – a decoration issued to warrant and junior officers of the army for exemplary gallantry in the presence of the enemy on land. On pressing Fairy more than 60 years later for more information, all he would tell me, with modesty equalling his bravery, was that he had been decorated for 'one or two actions in Indo-China'.

From Liverpool, my father travelled by train to London, then across to Victoria Station where he got on the wrong train and found himself in one of the Medway towns. Rather than waste time telephoning his parents, he jumped on a bus for Maidstone, walked through the town and up the hill, through the gate and up the garden path. Hearing a knock at the front door, my grandmother opened it to find herself staring at her elder son, who she had not seen for more than two years.

Any young man returning home after a few years away will have changed in some ways. To travel to India before the age of the jet would have been a rite of passage in itself, but to travel there and take part in conflict must have brought about some changes to a young person – some good, some bad. For my father, it brought an increased sense of duty, of honour and of pride in his country together with a deep interest in the people and places of other lands. It taught him to be respectful towards his superior officers while also being comfortable with those of both higher and lower rank than himself, and with those from different cultures. Fairy Gopsill described him as having an enormous sense of fun and a lightness of touch in any conversation – they all loved him. And of course he would draw cartoons to make them laugh. Had he not spent this time in India, he would undoubtedly have developed the same charming and enthusiastic personality but without the broader view, and without the discipline and attention to detail that he learned in the military and applied to everything he undertook thereafter in his professional career as an artist.

STEPPING OUT

Kneeling beside a huge sheet of yellow paper on the floor, Tony enlists the help of his accident-prone caretaker, Mr Bennett, to make a picture. He instructs Mr Bennett to put his foot into a tray of black paint, and then directs him in a sequence of footprints. With a hand on Tony's head to help keep his balance, Mr Bennett wisecracks his way across the paper, carefully placing his inky foot where Tony tells him. Several footprints run in a line, toe to heel, then more are placed side by side, and finally two more form an open V lying on its side.

Mr Bennett steps back to admire his handiwork – and accidentally puts one more print way off to the side of the paper. 'Don't worry, Mr Bennett,' says Tony, 'I can use that.' With a brush dipped in black paint, Tony adds a few lines and couple of curves to the lone print, creating a little figure that looks like a knight. He adds a great swirl of red, which emanates from the open V – and the lone figure has become a gallant St George brandishing his lance at a huge, fire-breathing dragon.

For the first time in three years, Tony stepped away from the control of the army, and began to get used to being his own master. Although he loved being in India, it was glorious to be back home in his own bed, with his own childhood things around him, and to revel in the fuss and attention lavished on him by his mother.

Thrilled to have their boy home, Tony's parents telephoned Clayesmore where brother Michael was now at school. Thinking that Tony would only be home on leave for a short while, they asked the school if Michael might be allowed home during term time to see him. This was duly granted, and the 17-year-old Michael travelled back to Maidstone.

During the previous school holidays, Michael had acquired a girlfriend, Pat, and he was desperate to show her off to Tony. 'Wear your uniform!' he instructed his brother. Pat was certainly impressed by this handsome young officer. So much so, in fact, that when Michael went back to school, Pat switched her allegiance from the younger brother to the elder.

So Tony's leave passed pleasantly with his new girlfriend, but before his leave was up he was contacted by the London regimental office and was surprised and disappointed to be told that he would not be returning to India. By this time, Partition had come fully into force and most of the British troops had withdrawn. Violence flared as Muslims were moved from India into Pakistan, and Hindus went in the opposite direction.

But Tony saw none of this; he was at home in Maidstone with his new girlfriend, and a prized possession: his Norton motorcycle. The Norton motorcycle was Tony's pride and joy. He perfected the knack of riding it up the front garden path, hitting the side gate with just enough force so that it swung open and allowed him to ride through, bounced against the wall and swung back with just enough momentum to close behind him and drop the latch. One evening, after a particularly happy time with Pat, he was riding home when he passed a sailor in uniform hitching a lift. Tony stopped. 'Where are you going?' he asked. 'Could you take me to the Dover road?' asked the sailor. Full of goodwill and in love with Pat and the rest of the world, my father cried, 'I'll take you to Dover! Jump on!' and proceeded to ride at breakneck speed all the way to the port. White-faced but grateful, the sailor shook his hand at Dover and tottered weakly away towards the safety of his ship.

There were all manner of opportunities for returning soldiers at that time. South Africa had a scheme to attract ex-soldiers into training as farmers, with a view to settling them there to farm the land. Fairy Gopsill had considered this himself, but his family had suggested that he might consider a career as a regular soldier. Within a month of returning home, Fairy received a signal from his regiment recommending that very thing, so he went back to pursue a career in the military. For my father, however, there was no prospect of returning to India, but there were opportunities for higher education. He enrolled at the Maidstone College of Art where he was to spend the next three years – and joined the Country Players, Maidstone's amateur dramatic society.

While he was at college, Tony spent a lot of time drawing from life. He went regularly to Maidstone Crown Court and drew what he saw there. One day, he watched the judge put on his black cap and saw a man receive the death penalty for murder. I asked him what the man's reaction was. 'Nothing,' replied my father. 'He was completely expressionless.' He was invited on one occasion to go down to the mortuary to draw a young woman who had drowned. 'She looks perfectly all right,' he was told, 'as if she was asleep.' But he couldn't bring himself to go.

It was at Maidstone that he perfected his craft. He had always been able to draw, and his art teacher at Clayesmore had improved his skill, but here he learned about other artists, the great masters, graphics and different ways of putting together pictures. The students were encouraged to draw nude models from life, who would pose for them for hours on end. They came in all shapes and sizes – old, young, ugly, attractive, thin and fat. One evening, a group of art students including my father attended a very smart party in London, and a woman in a stunning dress caught Tony's eye. On closer inspection, she turned out to be one of the models – and he had to admit that she looked a lot better with her clothes on.

Tony spent some time in the Department of Architecture, producing diagrammatic drawings of semi-detached houses, before spending the last two years of college in graphic design. While still at college, he was asked to produce a sign for the Maidstone County Show, and to design logos for farmers to put on their sacks. The students were also encouraged to teach art classes of their own, and my father found himself teaching children in a public school, patients in a mental hospital and – his personal favourite – the inmates of a prison.

Pat had by this time become my father's fiancée, but one day she appeared on the doorstep at Hastings Road to give him the news that she had met somebody else. Tony was dreadfully upset, and even more so when he found out that the man she wanted to marry was not only the son of the Lord Lieutenant of Kent, but also 41 years old. I did ask him what his brother had to say about all this, but Michael was away with the Lancashire Fusiliers at the time and so couldn't say anything.

With Pat out of his life, my father appeared with the Country Players one June as Puck in *A Midsummer Night's Dream*. Clad in nothing but a tiny pair of shorts embroidered with sycamore leaves, he delighted in playing Oberon's mischievous servant. The play was performed out of doors in the natural setting of Oakwood Park, and immediately behind the stage area, the ground dropped steeply away. When instructed to find the little flower, the juice of which would cause a comedy of errors, Tony's Puck replied, 'I go, I go,' then petulantly as Oberon turned away, '*Look* how I go! Swifter than arrow from the Tartar's bow!' whereupon he ran upstage, leapt high into the air and disappeared from sight, dropping some 15 feet straight down onto mattresses below. Tony's mother, my grandmother, must have thought a great deal of this performance, because she kept those little embroidered shorts and showed them to me many years later.

With college finished, and no ill will between them despite what had happened with Pat, Tony and Michael went to live in London, where they shared what my father described as a pretty grim basement flat in Kensington. Michael had been accepted as a drama student at the Webber Douglas School of Singing and Dramatic Art, and Tony was setting out as a struggling freelance artist.

One of his early jobs in 1950 was as a window display designer for Peter Robinson, a London department store in Leicester Square. There he met Yvonne Talbot who also worked in display, and together they would plan the window designs for the various departments. Yvonne told me that my father always arrived in the morning with a spring in his step and a smile on his face, always good humoured, ready and eager to get to the drawing board. She remembers him being very proud of his time with the Gurkha Rifles and that he often drew on his experiences in India, incorporating them into his designs. Yvonne particularly remembers one of his windows, which they named 'King Solomon's Mines' and which incorporated those brilliant colours so evocative of India, attracting a lot of attention.

The store regularly held inter-departmental competitions for the best-dressed window, and Tony teamed himself up with a window dresser from the lingerie department. They put their heads together and came up with a brilliant idea. Their window took the form of a cell in a monastery, with a cartoon monk holding up his hands in shock and horror, for flying around the room, looking for all the world like a flock of bats, were multitudes of black lacy knickers and brassieres. Naturally, their window won.

An artist's life had a few perks. Around this time Tony was commissioned to paint a mural on the wall of a restaurant, Abbotts in Kensington. The mural was of a cartoon abbot, and many years later my father recreated him on the wall of his old film shed at the cottage in Surrey. Instead of being paid a fee for the job, he was given supper and told to come and have a meal whenever he wanted to. Although he was not quite starving in a garret, Tony could get pretty hungry in his basement and he took up this invitation of a meal on more than one occasion.

One evening in 1952, his brother Michael invited Tony to a party held by one of his friends from the Webber Douglas, and it was here that my father met a BBC television producer. As luck would have it, the producer was looking for someone who could draw cartoon illustrations for his programme *Saturday Special*. 'Can you draw quickly?' he asked. Seizing a napkin, Tony rapidly drew a fish blowing bubbles and without further ado the job was his.

The programme, which was an entertaining and informative show for children featuring stories, puppetry and comic sketches, was broadcast live every week from the BBC's Lime Grove studios in Shepherd's Bush. Working alongside several aspiring young entertainers including Peter Butterworth, Harry Corbett and Sooty, my father found himself making models and producing drawings to illustrate the stories for the programme. On one occasion, Tony had not finished the last illustration before it was required, so he finished drawing it live on air. The producer liked this, and so from then on each one was drawn live on camera – with just my father's hand in shot. But one day he leaned in too close, and his head appeared as well. Fortunately, the producer liked this too, and Tony Hart the TV artist was born.

Originally built by the Gaumont Film Company in 1915, Lime Grove Studios was a rabbit warren of studios and corridors, and in the 1950s home to such early television programmes as *Tonight*, *What's My Line* and *Dixon of Dock Green*. For the younger viewer, Lime Grove was the birthplace of many children's programmes, including the puppets of *Andy Pandy*, *Bill and Ben*, *Whirligig* and *The Woodentops*. Lime Grove was a residential road with, looking somewhat out of place, a large television studio building in the middle of it. Passing through a corridor between two of the studios on one of the upper levels heading towards the design department, it was bizarre but captivating to find the designer's offices located in what had obviously been the bedrooms of the terraced houses behind, and which had been knocked through to form part of the studios themselves – winding staircases, fireplaces, dormer windows and all. There was very much a family atmosphere at Lime Grove in those early days, and everyone knew everybody else. Nobody quite knew what they were supposed to be doing in those early, pioneering days of television – mostly they were making it up as they went along, and there always seemed to be time to stop for a chat. One swelteringly hot summer's day one of the children's production teams, seeking a cooler working environment, moved their office furniture outside on to a balcony which had recently been surfaced with tarmac. After a few hours, the team was dismayed to find that in the heat, their metal chairs had gradually sunk into the soft tarmac and stuck fast.

The programmes made at Lime Grove shared studios; *Saturday Special* shared their studio with *Tonight*, a live current affairs programme broadcast on weekday evenings and presented by Cliff Michelmore. An item in one *Saturday Special* programme involved several cut-out objects which were sticky on the reverse, enabling my father to stick them onto a mounted board which made up part of the set and move them around if necessary. One of these was an umbrella which, unnoticed at the end of the programme, got knocked off its board. During the scene change while the studio was being made ready for Cliff's programme and the *Tonight* set was being put up, one of the scene-shifters picked up the umbrella and slapped it carelessly on to the set behind Cliff's chair, which that week included a picture of a Chinese mandarin. Completely unaware of this addition to their set, the *Tonight* programme broadcast its usual mixture of current affairs, arts, sciences and topical matters while behind Cliff the audience was puzzled to see an image of a Chinese mandarin with an umbrella sticking out of his ear. Although the first appearance of Tony's cut-out umbrella was accidental, it became a standing joke and went on to make several subsequent appearances on charts, on maps and even on Cliff's desk – assuming mascot status with the *Tonight* team. Years later when entertaining an audience, Tony would often produce a drawing to illustrate this tale.

Generally, after broadcasting their programmes, the production teams would frequent the pub on the corner of Lime Grove; the *Saturday Special* team was no exception. Tony had often noticed an attractive young woman in there, also from the BBC, drinking with the *Whirligig* production team. He had been briefly introduced to her once before and knew her name was Jean. On this particular evening, having finished broadcasting *Saturday Special* – a memorable occasion that included an item with a llama which had upset the floor manager by peeing all over the studio – Tony went to the pub and saw the young woman having a drink with two men. One was a producer whom he knew slightly, and the other was the owner of La Lanterne, a Soho restaurant. He spoke with them briefly, and then left them to push his way through the smoky throng to join two up-and-coming young actors he knew standing at the bar – Harry Secombe and Eric Sykes – but all the while covertly watching the group of three. After a while, the two men went to get their coats, but the young woman was looking uncertain. My father went over to her and asked if she was all right. She told him that her producer had said to her that she ought to go and have dinner with the Soho restaurant owner. 'Do you want to go?' asked Tony. 'No, I don't,' she replied. 'Then,' said my father firmly, 'you are not having dinner with him, you are having dinner with me.' A year later they were married.

My parent's wedding in 1953 was not entirely conventional. The congregation was small, just immediate friends and family, as was the reception party that followed in their Richmond flat. I remember my father telling me that the organ in the church was broken, so Jean walked up the aisle to a piano accompaniment wearing, in a total departure from convention, a dramatic dark red taffeta dress with a huge collar and plunging neckline. Tony was sure that as they knelt before the altar, the vicar had a spectacular view down the front of my mother's dress. There was no official photographer, so press pictures are the only record of this happy event.

At the party afterwards, my parents' television background was reflected in more than one of the congratulatory telegrams that were read out to the assembled guests.

A friend of theirs, scriptwriter Peter Ling, sent this message: 'Fade in FX wedding bells. Sorry I had to track out, but best wishes on your two shot. Mix to years of future happiness. Cue grams Wedding March. Love Peter Ling.'

Humphrey Lestocq, the presenter of *Whirligig*, sent a pithier message: 'Here's hoping for a nice long run and successful first night. HL.'

Tony and Jean loved their little flat on the Courtlands estate in Richmond. Although they struggled to make ends meet on my mother's regular salary as a production secretary, topped up from time to time with my father's freelance earnings, those early days in their marriage were mostly happy ones. My father admitted to me many years later, however, that he hated it when my mother went away filming as she frequently did when working on the BBC's detective drama *Maigret*. She was a good-looking girl, and he was convinced that she would run into somebody else better looking and wealthier than him. This unfounded paranoia came to a head one evening when my mother returned home very late one rainy night having been away for several days. It was so late that the trains had stopped running and one of the members of the film unit had been unable to get home, so my mother had suggested that he spend the night on the sofa at their flat. When my father, who had been waiting up, saw that she had brought a man home with her, he became instantly so blinded with jealous rage that without waiting for any explanation he threw the unfortunate chap straight out into the rain and darkness. My mother was not impressed, and relations were a little frosty for a short while. On recounting this tale, Pa ruefully admitted that his behaviour was not only inexcusable but downright rude – a trait he abhorred in anybody.

My father's bedroom studio in their Richmond flat was a busy place in those early days of television. *In Town Tonight* was a topical magazine programme broadcast live by the BBC on Saturday nights in the 1950s, featuring interviews with well-known stars and celebrities of the day. As each interviewee was introduced, viewers at home were fascinated by a whirling image that appeared on the screen, featuring cartoons which had been drawn by my father. The list of guests would be telephoned through to him on the Thursday afternoon before transmission, and Pa would immediately set to work on drawing if not a caricature of the guest, then something appropriate, on a disc of card; sometimes he had to race around to find a photograph to work from. Come transmission, the disc was rotated on a turntable and filmed through a special camera lens, giving a moving kaleidoscope effect. Invariably though, there would be a last-minute guest, and the drawing to introduce them would have to be done in the studio. On one occasion, the last-minute guest was Jean Kent, a British film actress. The production team had acquired a photograph of her and thinking this would do, had stuck it on to the disc, but during rehearsal the glossy print was reflecting too much light and flaring badly. So with minutes to go before transmission, the glamorous film star sat for my Pa while he rapidly made a drawing of her – using as always black pen and white pencil on grey card, which worked best for black-and-white television – and fixed it to the disc just in time for the start of the programme. On another occasion, a Russian singer was due to appear, but for some reason the Soviet Embassy decided to pull him out of the programme just 20 minutes before transmission. As an instant replacement, the production team dragged in a Texan cowboy with his guitar from the nearest variety theatre, but of course my father had already prepared the disc featuring a Russian figure and the Red Star – which would have made no sense for introducing the Texan. Swiftly he amended his design by turning the Red Star into a Texan Star, added a guitar to the Russian figure and put a lasso into its hand – and slid it onto the turntable with seconds to spare.

On rare occasions, my mother found herself getting involved with my father's work in those early days. He had been asked to come up with a filmed title sequence for a story entitled '1600 Feet Under the Sea', and had decided that a stretch of dark water draining away to reveal letters spelling out the title underneath would be effective. Computer graphic imaging was nonexistent in those days, and special effects were also pretty rudimentary, so he achieved his concept by sticking the letters making up the title on the bottom of a black photographic dish in which he had made a small hole. With the camera fixed directly above the dish, and my mother's finger blocking the hole, he filled the dish with black inky water, and then, with my mother removing her finger on cue, filmed the water draining away to reveal the title. Brilliant!

During this time, my father met a man who was to become a close friend for the rest of his life – indeed, his wife Joan in due course became my godmother. His name was Ron Massara, and he was the banqueting manager at the Hyde Park Hotel in Knightsbridge. A struggling artist like my father did not patronise the Hyde Park as a rule, but he and my mother were often taken there as guests by a cousin of the then Prime Minister, Anthony Eden. He was an elderly gentleman who had taken a shine to the young couple, and they to him, but he had one very odd custom. They would meet at his flat for a drink before going on to the Hyde Park, and he would insist on cleaning out their noses with water pumped from a syringe. My father said it was marvellous, cleaned everything out and left you feeling fresh and revitalized. My mother on the other hand told me that it was most peculiar but didn't suppose it did any harm. The ritual complete, the party of three would make their way through Knightsbridge to the Hyde Park.

They had been introduced to Massara (as he was always known) on previous visits, but on this occasion the friend they were with had had a little more to drink than usual before dinner and wasn't holding it well. He informed their waiter who had come to take their order that he wanted scrambled eggs and spaghetti. The waiter politely told him that they would not serve scrambled eggs with spaghetti and the older man became excitable and began to shout. From the other side of the restaurant, Massara saw this heated exchange and swiftly came across to calm the situation. Having mollified the titled gentleman by suggesting an acceptable alternative to scrambled eggs and spaghetti, he turned his attention to my father. On discovering he was a TV artist, he asked if he could design a logo to be used on the menu for a convention of doctors, due shortly to hold their event at the hotel. On the back of a menu card, Tony quickly sketched a little cartoon character with a black bag and a stethoscope, which met with Massara's instant approval.

Over the years, my father went on to design many menu cards for Massara but was never paid with money. Instead, he and my mother – and later me as well – would be treated to dinner and a suite for the night at the Hyde Park, and be sent away with a case of wine or champagne. My mother always said that because of this, they developed a taste for fine wine early on that far exceeded their income.

My father very much enjoyed fine food and wine, but he equally enjoyed the simpler things. He had told me about salt beef sandwiches, and how the best ones could only be found in specific sandwich bars in London. I was keen to try one of these, and pressed the matter on our next visit to the Hyde Park. My father said, 'All right, but for heaven's sake don't tell Massara or he'll be offended.' We arrived at the hotel mid-afternoon, and when Massara asked if we wanted afternoon tea to be sent up to our suite, my father replied, 'No, we'll save ourselves for dinner.' Once we were sure Massara was safely back in his little office, we sneaked down the back stairs and furtively made our way out through a side door – probably drawing far more attention to ourselves than if we had simply walked out through the main foyer. We rapidly disappeared into the back streets of Knightsbridge and found a sandwich bar where we sat up on high stools at the counter and ate the most delicious hot salt beef sandwiches made with wonderfully soft white bread. This was every bit as enjoyable as, and contrasted spectacularly with, our dinner later that evening in the Grill Room at the Hyde Park, with a four-piece band playing soft music, glasses and china sparkling in the candlelight, and the immaculate waiters tending to the needs of the diners under the watchful eye of the tall and elegant Massara.

In 1974 on his retirement, a party was held in Massara's honour, and my father produced a series of cartoons for him chronicling his career as a hotelier. One of these illustrated an event that occurred shortly after the Second World War when Massara was trying to make something of the Hyde Park Hotel, which at that time was a huge, rambling, run-down Victorian building complete with rats. Apparently unaware of the state of the hotel, a titled couple decided to hold their silver wedding party there, and their glittering guest list included King George VI and Queen Elizabeth. Realising that this royal visit could put the Hyde Park back on the map, Massara went to enormous lengths to make up for the poor state of the hotel and put on a party fit for a king. As the hotel china was cracked, he borrowed some Doulton china from a department store for the night; Joan, his wife, hand-sewed the serviettes – since post-war, items of this kind were in short supply; he covered the holes in the threadbare carpets with rugs borrowed from Harvey Nichols, the department store across the road; he managed to source impossible items such as white toilet paper; he hired a band to play during the meal; and he borrowed top waiters from other London hotels and restaurants. His efforts were well rewarded – the party went so well that when dinner was over and the band was still playing, the King asked if the carpets could be rolled up so that the assembled company could dance. Although anxious that the state of the carpets would be revealed, Massara of course agreed to the request and found himself directing operations while the delighted King abandoned protocol and lent a hand with rolling up the carpets. Nearly three decades later at Massara's retirement party, one of several cartoons drawn by my father illustrates this particular story – which in turn illustrates his own attention to detail and lightness of touch as we see, on a coat-stand behind the royal couple rolling up the carpets, the King's dinner jacket and, hanging beside it, a crown.

It was after an evening at the Hyde Park that my father had the second experience of his lifetime in which a few hours were lost to him. Unlike the events in India where shock and the reaction to a situation had caused him to drink excessively, nothing untoward had happened in the Grill Room that night; he'd been having a lovely time. Bottle after convivial bottle arrived and was consumed with enormous enjoyment in warm and genial company as the evening went on and on. But Pa does not remember leaving the Hyde Park, and, appallingly, he certainly doesn't remember driving home to Esher – which he must have done since at the time my mother couldn't drive. He does, however, remember the dreadful hangover he had the next morning, and the cure for it which he later recommended to me – a fizzing concoction of water with a couple of aspirin dissolved in it for the head, an Alka-Seltzer for the stomach, and a spoonful of glucose for a boost of energy.

As a freelance artist, work for my father at this time came in fits and starts, but with my mother working as well, they were just about able to make ends meet whenever Pa was having a quiet patch. In the late 1950s, my mother would go to work looking very smart in a short coat, high heels and gloves, but when she went away filming, she opted for rather more comfortable slacks with flat shoes and a raincoat. One afternoon having just returned from a few days away filming, the telephone rang. It was the local police station to say that our dog, a wire-haired terrier that rejoiced in the name of Baggy, had been found wandering by someone who had brought her into the police station. Would my mother come down and pick her up? It was pouring with rain, and the coat my mother had been wearing was completely sodden, so she picked up a grubby old mackintosh that she wore on wet days in the garden and which had a large rip in the sleeve and one or two buttons missing.

By the time she got to the police station, she was a sorry sight in her scruffy coat with her hair plastered down over her face and water pouring out of her shoes. My mother approached the tired-looking sergeant behind the desk, but before she could state her business there was a resounding crash from somewhere at the back of the police station. The sergeant heaved a sigh and followed the source of the crash saying wearily, 'And what have you done now?' The object of his attention was, of course, our dog, who had been having a wonderful time chasing around the police station and sticking her nose into everything that didn't concern her. My mother announced that she had come to collect the animal, and with another heavy sigh, the sergeant scooped Baggy up in his arms and put her on the desk saying, 'That'll be a shilling.' Then he looked closely at my wreck of a mother and asked doubtfully, 'Have you got a shilling?' Fortunately she had, having stuffed her purse into her pocket on the way out, and Baggy, having been thus bailed, returned home after her illicit wanderings. As it was one of their better financial periods, my father was amused when my mother, recounting the story, told him that the desk sergeant had thought she might be destitute.

TONY HART – A PORTRAIT OF MY DAD

As a freelance artist, it was always a worry wondering where the next job was coming from, but from *Saturday Special*, Tony went straight on to join the *Playbox* team. Hosted by Eamonn Andrews, *Playbox* was a family show with a quiz element featuring two teams of young contestants, and also included the talents of Cliff Michelmore, Rolf Harris and Johnny Morris who, as the Hot Chestnut Man, told stories and voiced the characters that appeared in his tales – a precursor to his talking animals in *Animal Magic*. Tony's contribution was, of course, to draw captions as clues to the questions for the young teams. For each programme, he would only have a rough idea of what line the questions were going to take – songs or proverbs or sayings, and so he would be drawing the caption clues off the cuff. Not being a great pop fan, the music clues could sometimes puzzle him, but at the end of every programme the children would always rush for the drawings to take them home.

Eamonn was to become a close friend. I remember going to Eamonn's house as a very little girl with my parents, and the house was full of partying grown-ups. Total tedium was relieved by a young Hayley Mills, who sat on the hearthrug with me and played cat's cradle. It was at Eamonn's house that Tony got to meet a long-time hero of his, the writer and broadcaster Patrick Campbell. Eamonn knew my father was keen to meet Patrick, and when he arrived, he gestured over the noisy throng, pointing right then left, then straight up. Puzzled, Tony walked through the corridor to the right, then left into the drawing room and looked up to find himself gazing at the extremely tall Patrick Campbell who towered over the group of people he was entertaining by a head. Happily, my father needed no introduction as Patrick recognized him immediately – which is just as well since his well-known and much played upon stammer would have made it impossible for him to greet my father by his name!

The *Playbox* series ran for five years, and my father's next programme was *Ask Your Dad*, another children's quiz show featuring two teams of children, each team having a 'dad' to whom they could appeal for help if they were unable to answer the questions posed by the chairman. My father not only designed the title card for the series, but was also one of the 'dads' doing his best to assist his young team – he was invaluable on questions of general knowledge, but of little help when the question was about pop music. The other dad, who was worth his weight in gold for any question on sport, was the well-known cricketing commentator who was to become a good friend of my father's, Brian Johnston.

By this time, along with his television work, Tony was drawing a cartoon strip for the *TV Comic*, a children's magazine. Drawn from his experiences in India, the two main characters were Tipu, a little Indian boy, and Packi, a white elephant – his name derived from the word 'pachyderm', being a thick-skinned quadruped, or elephant. Packi and Tipu enjoyed many adventures together; the storyline for the children was captioned below each illustration, and the speech bubbles within the drawing could sometimes contain a rather more sophisticated humour. In one adventure where they were making their way through dense jungle, Packi and Tipu encountered an Englishman in a safari suit armed with a butterfly net. Tipu's speech bubble announced, 'Dr Attenbrolly, I presume?' These four words are a lovely example of my father's ability to incorporate cultural references into his art, in a witty and charming way. Not only does this echo the immortal words uttered by journalist Henry Stanley on finding Dr Livingstone in a remote African village in 1871, it also acknowledges the up-and-coming young naturalist David Attenborough. Packi and Tipu graduated from comics to television, and in 1960, the drawings for 'Packi and Tipu and the Windmill' were among the very first to appear as a captioned story on television. Drawn in black and white on grey paper some of these illustrations were very wide, allowing the camera to pan across the picture, giving some movement to the images.

Since his days at art college, my father had from time to time been asked to design logos. In 1958, he was asked by the BBC to design a logo for a new children's programme that was to be called *Blue Peter*. More than fifty years later that programme is still running today and still uses his design: the iconic *Blue Peter* ship. He was asked what sort of fee he wanted for this, and wondered if a penny for every time it was shown would be a good idea. 'Don't think that'll amount to very much,' he was told. 'What about £100?' A hundred pounds in the late fifties was a perfectly acceptable fee, and there was no way of knowing how successful the programme was going to be. But, with hindsight, a penny a time wouldn't have been a bad deal at all!

So by leaving the British army in India, the young officer stepped away from the protective shield of the military, and allowed his creative gene to thrive for the next three years within the conclaves of Maidstone Art College – and within another three had taken massive strides towards becoming a household name.

In India, he used his artistic talent but little – drawing principally for his friends to make them laugh. When I met his Commanding Officer many years later, I asked this man if he had known about my father's drawing skills. 'Not really,' he replied with a smile, 'we kept him much too busy for any of that.' And although my father never returned to India – something that he thought at one time in later life he might like to do but was afraid that he might find it too much changed – he drew upon the colours and images and styles that he had seen there throughout his career.

College sharpened and honed his talent and this, combined with his exceptional skill, a wonderful ease of personality and an enormous enthusiasm for everything he undertook, endeared him to everyone he met. And my father's involvement with amateur dramatics should not be dismissed lightly, as this gave him invaluable experience of performing in front of an audience.

Here then was a precocious bubble of talent with an infectious charm and enthusiasm and, growing at the same time, was a new and fast-developing visual medium of broadcasting – television. It was perhaps inevitable that the two should collide in an explosion of picture-making. But more than this, it was the combination of the two that went on to form the benchmark for the children's art programmes that appear on our screens to this day.

ITALIAN MARBLE

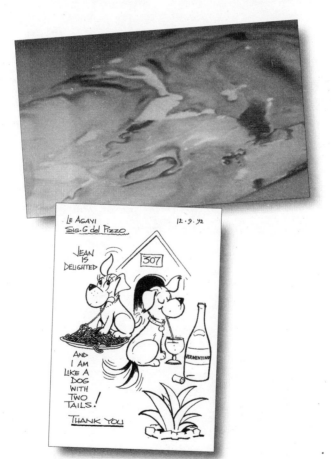

Tony takes a shallow tray and fills it with clean water – emphasising that it must be clean. Then he takes a tube of blue oil paint and squeezes some paint into the water. Immediately, the paint contorts itself into swirls and loops and convoluted shapes as it struggles but fails to combine with the water. Tony tells us we can give it a stir, or just simply blow into the tray – which he does – and immediately the patterns become even more intricate. Taking a piece of plain white paper, he lays this briefly on the surface of the water and, lifting it off, reveals a print of a fantastic marbled design.

Early on in their married life, before I was born, Tony and Jean discovered Italy, and their love for that country, its people and its food and wine, lasted all of their lives. Despite visits to many other countries, Italy remained their favourite place to rest and relax. It was my mother who discovered this jewel of the Mediterranean. She was a member of the English Speaking Union, an organisation whose remit was, and still is, to promote 'international understanding and friendship through the use of the English language'. In their newsletter she had found an advertisement for a small hotel – or *pensione* – run by an English couple in Sori, a little village on the north-western coast tucked between Genoa and Portofino. Enchanted by the description of the place, Tony and Jean made their reservations and took their car on a Bristol Freighter, a small prop-engine aircraft that took just nine passengers and three cars, from Lydd in Kent to Le Touquet, and then drove down through France, over the Simplon and then into Italy.

Incidentally, it was at Le Touquet airport that my mother made a spectacular exhibition of herself on one occasion. The wind was gusty, and she was wearing, as fashion in the mid-fifties demanded, a very full skirt. My father had wandered off to check on the car, the crew was standing by the aircraft, and my mother was touching

59

up her lipstick using her powder compact mirror. With both hands occupied, there was nothing she could do about a sudden gust of wind that blew her skirt right up over her head. She fought with it for some moments, and, having got the front of the skirt under some semblance of control during a brief lull in the wind, she found she had an admiring audience in the shape of the aircraft crew. As her skirt flew up again with another gust, she called to them crossly, 'Don't just stand there – come and help me!'

The journey to Italy took three days, and they would stop somewhere around Reims to buy provisions for a picnic lunch and then find a pretty place to stop and eat and have a pee. I know this, because in 1965 I went with them for the first time. My mother's job was to go and find bread, cheese and wine, while my father would go off in search of a charcuterie to buy vast quantities of saucisson sec – a dried sausage of which he was particularly fond. Then they would drive out into the countryside to find a suitably idyllic spot in which to eat. On my first trip with my parents, I enjoyed the food shopping, but must confess that it was the peeing bit I found difficult. For Tony, an al fresco pee of course presented no problem whatsoever, nor for Jean who had had some practice at this. But at eight years old I was not used to peeing outdoors, and was in severe danger of getting lost as I took myself so far off in order to avoid being seen by anybody; and keeping shoes and socks dry while crouching awkwardly behind the thickest patch of scrub to avoid detection and stretching my knickers to their limit to keep them out of the stream of wee was well nigh impossible. I would eventually rejoin my parents having wandered around in circles for several minutes before finding my way back to our picnic spot with either damp drawers or damp shoes, or both. I'm still no good at it. However, in those early years on their own, I'm sure my parents had no trouble in this regard.

They would drive on to Chaumont and stay at the Hotel de la

Gare where they delighted in eating snails followed by steak, cooked *bleu*. (This was a taste I acquired early on, and when I accompanied them and asked for escargots and a filet bleu, the waiter blinked and asked my parents if I was sure. 'She's sure,' my mother replied, and the waiters, who had hitherto held themselves somewhat aloof, condescended to smile benignly upon this little *anglaise* who, it seemed, knew how to enjoy French food.) From Chaumont, Tony and Jean would drive up into the Alps and stay overnight at the Simplon Hotel. I was enchanted with this place the first time I saw it: a proper wooden chalet, beds made up with duvets (almost unheard of in the UK at that time), an enormous stuffed bear (real) in the entrance hall, the clonking sound of the cow bells up in the pastures, and the mountains wearing swathes of white alabaster rock on their shoulders which looked like snow. My father and I would try and walk to the real snow, which was higher up and looked so close, but we could never reach it. The next day, it was a short drive down the mountain and across the border into Italy.

The hotel was called Villa Le Rondini – 'The Swallow'. It was a large pink villa with green shutters perched high on the hillside overlooking the terraced vineyards and the roofs of the faded pink and yellow houses of Sori, with the glittering Mediterranean beyond. Le Rondini had previously been owned by the English Gye family since 1890, and much of the old Florentine furniture remained – giving the villa a flavour of stately, if somewhat faded, opulence. Fresh vegetables, oranges, figs, olives, grapes and tangerines were grown in the gardens, and used to good effect in the kitchen. Le Rondini's little brochure stated: 'All the amenities of the Villa are reserved for en pension guests only, and thus the staff are at their entire disposal at any season,' which sums up the air of gracious gentility which my mother and father so enjoyed there.

Le Rondini had its own private bit of coast, but there was no beach, only rocky platforms which were reached by more than 100 steps leading down through the terraces from the villa, and from which you had to dive or jump off straight into deep water. Sometimes the sea was very rough, with waves crashing over the rocks, completely submerging the lower platform and sending spray up over the second platform some 20 feet higher. On the lower platform, there was a stone seat carved into the rock face with an iron bar set like a grab-rail on either side.

On one blisteringly hot day, on that first visit to Sori with my parents, I looked longingly at the azure sea, but it was too rough to go in. In an attempt to cool off, Pa and I went down and sat on the higher platform, letting the spray from the waves hit us, but the sun was so hot that the spray did little to cool us down. Then my father had a plan. We watched the sea carefully, and it seemed that there were about ten seconds between each big wave. 'Come on,' he said. 'When I say "go" we'll run down to the platform and sit on the stone seat – ready? Go!' We galloped down the rocks and jumped down on to the stone platform, being careful not to slip on the wet rock, and skidded on to the stone seat. My father held on to one of the iron bars and reached across me to hold the other, pinning me against the rock and turning himself into a human seatbelt. As we faced the sea, a huge wave was forming in front of us. 'Hold your breath and hang on!' cried Pa. I took a deep breath and the great wave crashed over both of us, soaking and cooling us from head to foot. It tried to suck us back into the sea, but my father had me securely braced against the rock. We stayed there for about ten minutes, gasping as wave after wave bashed its way over us, forcing our backs hard against the rough face of the rock and then trying to drag us off and down into the foaming depths. At last he said, 'When I say "go", we run back up, OK?' 'OK!' I shouted as another wave exploded over our heads. 'Go!' shouted my father as it began to suck its way back over the rocky platform. He let go of the iron bar, releasing me, and we ran duck-footed over the wet stone so as not to slip. We leapt like mountain goats up the rocks to the safety of the upper level where we threw ourselves down, panting and laughing. Eventually, we made our way back up to the Rondini and found my mother sitting sweatily in the shade of a grapevine on the verandah. Observing our wet and bedraggled appearance she said, 'Good Lord, you haven't been in, have you?' Pa and I grinned at each other. 'Kind of!' he said.

On their very first visit to Le Rondini, Tony and Jean had arrived late for dinner and instead of being led to their own table in the restaurant, they were instantly separated and sat at a large table with about 12 other people. At first they were horrified but quickly discovered that the other guests at Le Rondini were like-minded people – among them George Martin, now world-famous for his work with the sixties pop group The Beatles and many, many others. This of course was the very early sixties, and George at this time was relatively unknown. With him was Judy, who on that visit was not yet his wife. The elderly James and Olivia Gye, the English couple who ran Le Rondini, were somewhat puritanical of spirit and insisted on giving George his own room – which was situated above the laundry some distance away down in the village.

At this time, my mother and father and their friends were all in their twenties or early thirties, all of them young professionals, intelligent and fun-loving. Among them was Jeremy Gye, James and Olivia's son who helped his parents with the running of the hotel – the kitchen being his main domain. One day at lunchtime Jeremy, sitting at one end of the large table, asked George, sitting at the other, to pass a dish of onions. George spooned an onion out of the dish and looked askance at Jeremy. Jeremy said 'Go on, I'll catch it!' George catapulted the onion the length of the table, Jeremy missed it and it hit the wall behind him with a loud splat and slid slowly downwards. James and Olivia were unimpressed, while the rest of the assembled company roared with laughter. For the most part, however, James and Olivia were obviously happy with their guests. If people didn't quite fit, they had a way of making them not exactly unwelcome, but they were not encouraged to return. Tony, Jean, George and Judy, however, went back again and again.

One of my father's favourite memories is of a warm evening sitting out on the terrace under the vine leaves after dinner with coffee and liqueurs, watching the twinkling lights of the village of Camogli appearing along the coast as darkness fell, and listening to the air throb with the sound of cicadas. George and Judy had just arrived from England where George had been working with The Beatles, and had brought a new vinyl recording with him. Assuming it was a Beatles record, Jeremy found an old record player from somewhere and put it on. But instead of loud pop music, out into this magical Italian dusk floated what was to become one of my father's favourite pieces of music – the shamelessly romantic theme that George had composed for the film *Elizabeth and Essex*.

My parents returned to Le Rondini year after year – sometimes twice in one year – sometimes meeting old friends there; often making new ones. One such, Barry Chapman, remembers an occasion out on the sunny verandah after everyone, including a number of visiting children, had been swimming, and tea and biscuits were being served. The children had been pressing the grown-ups for the meaning of various words, and one of them asked the meaning of onomatopoeia. 'Hang on a minute,' said my father and promptly went inside the villa. For a moment nothing happened, and then a doormat was flung out on to the verandah, followed seconds later by Pa himself, who leaped through the open doorway and landed on the doormat announcing, 'I, on a mat, appear!'

Because of my father's work commitments and my schooling, I was only able to accompany them to Le Rondini three times while I was growing up. I was eight years old the first time I went, and I just loved it. Olivia Gye had died a few years previously and my parents told me to be extremely polite to James, as they had been led to believe that he was not particularly fond of children. So, already an enthusiastic student of the Tony Hart charm school, I put myself on my best behaviour and James and I got on like a house on fire. Each evening, we would all rendezvous in the Rondini's little bar, and I would always find myself to be the first one down. While I perched on a bar stool, James would pour for me the most delicious peach drink complete with ice and a straw. Pa would be the next one down – his face an interesting shade of lobster due to a touch of sunburn combined with his usual blazing hot bath. He was surprised and delighted on our first evening to find James and I deep in friendly conversation.

I loved the food – in 1965, although there were separate tables for guests at the Rondini by this time, there was no menu and you ate what you were given and it was superb. I was introduced to Italian food in all its glory – pasta, pizza, fish, cheese and oh the fruit! Huge white sweet and juicy peaches, and fat purple figs which Pa taught me to eat by cutting a cross in them and then squeezing so that the four quarters opened up like a flower allowing me to suck out the delicious red seeds. He also introduced me to another gastronomic delight essential to a child – Italian ice cream.

On that first visit, we left my mother behind to lie on the rocks in the sun, and drove along the coast to Santa Margherita to a restaurant run by two brothers whom my father knew well. We sat outside on the terrace, exotic with palm trees and geraniums, overlooking the sparkling sea. After introducing me to the brothers and explaining that this was my first visit to Italy, they produced a great frosted goblet of a dish filled with chocolate, coffee and vanilla ice-cream, finished with chocolate sauce and nuts and adorned with biscuits and wafers. I had never tasted anything so wonderful in my life.

Our days were spent swimming from the rocks – my mother inseparable from her rubber ring – visiting the little towns along the coast, lying in the sun reading our books and eating and drinking. Somewhere on our journey between Le Touquet and Sori, we had acquired a blow-up dinghy from one of the petrol stations, and I spent a great deal of time rowing it about in the sea. On one occasion, I suggested that we all get in it, and there followed a lengthy and inelegant interlude while the Hart family attempted to board this unstable but gallant little vessel.

Because of their many visits to Le Rondini, my parents made several friends in the area. One of them was a tall dark Englishman called Shane who taught English at the university in Milan, and on who, during my second visit to Italy at the age of 12, I developed something of a crush. Shane lived in a small apartment perched high on the hillside overlooking the Mediterranean, which had a small terraced garden surrounded by a wild tangle of pink roses. It was while we were sitting on the terrace eating salami and raw broad beans by way of an antipasto that a gum boil I had been cultivating for a day or two suddenly burst. My face obviously registered the horrible taste of burst boil in my mouth and Pa immediately realised what had happened. He demanded of Shane a large glass of warm salty water and led me to the edge of the terrace, encouraging me to sloosh and spit over the railing and down onto the hillside below. This I did with as much grace as I could muster, which wasn't much, horribly aware that I was probably not making the greatest impression upon our tall, dark and handsome host.

I was 15 on my third and last visit. Both James and Olivia Gye were gone by this time and Jeremy had taken over the entire running of the hotel. One evening after dinner, my mother, my father and I decided to take a stroll down into the village. I was lagging a little behind my parents, and as we reached the village square two handsome young men approached me and began to speak in rapid Italian. I shrugged helplessly stammering, 'Non parlo Italiano' – which I couldn't apart from yes, no, please and thank you and, wildly useful as a result of reading the notice on the back of the bathroom door on a daily basis, 'please do not throw rubbish of any sort down this lavatory' – which hardly seemed an appropriate thing to say to the young men.

Realising that I had fallen behind, my mother turned back and came to the rescue by pointing to me and then to herself and announcing 'Inglese'. They gabbled at her, and she picked up the word *ballo*. Turning to my father she said, 'I think they're inviting Carolyn to a dance.' My father looked unimpressed. 'I don't think that's a very good idea,' he said. The young men looked at each other and then gabbled some more, gesturing at my mother. She laughed and turning again to my father said, 'They're saying they'll take me along too if you'll let Carolyn go.' Pa was outraged. 'Certainly not!' he barked, and promptly led his womenfolk at a brisk march out of the square back towards the pensione. 'Did you want to go?' inquired my mother as we walked up the road. Being only just 15 and not speaking the language, I had to admit that although hugely flattered, no, I wouldn't have wanted to. Pa nodded his approval at this as we walked through the Mediterranean dusk up the vine-covered driveway and into the safety of Le Rondini.

My parents' love affair with Italy lasted all through the 50 years of their married life. When eventually Le Rondini was sold to new owners, they tried Sicily and Crete as holiday destinations, but neither compared with Italy. So after a three-year gap, they returned once again to Italy, this time travelling further south where they promptly fell in love with Positano, a town almost surreal in its charm that clings to the mountain rising from the Mediterranean just south of the Bay of Naples. For many years in succession they stayed at the Royal Hotel and then, when it was taken over for development into apartments, they discovered Le Agavi, a jewel of a hotel with its balconies and terraces that string their way down the mountainside to the sea. For more than 20 years, they visited the Agavi every June and October to lie in the sun, swim and eat, forging close friendships with the management and staff. In Guglielmo's – the manager's – office hangs to this day a cartoon drawn by Pa with a caption which sums up one of their early holidays there: 'Jean is delighted, and I am like a dog with two tails!' Usually they went for two weeks, and occasionally three, and my father always used to say it took a week for his toes to stop twitching and he could begin to relax.

And a well-earned relaxation it was when you consider his workload in any one season. Aside from all the personal appearances at local schools and shopping centres, there were illustrations to be done for other people's books, designs to be created for charities, captions to be made for other people's television programmes – and then there were his own. Thirteen television programmes made up a series of both *Take Hart* and *Hart Beat*, and each programme included four designs – one for the younger viewers under seven, one for the older ones over ten, and two for the main target audience of the seven- to ten-year-olds in between, and all of them researched and tried and tested before ever reaching a television studio. An example of some of the diverse materials he would use in a single series would include paper straws, molten wax, pasta, clay, sandpaper, chalk, garden wire, toilet rolls, salt, egg shells, Chinese brushes and moss. He was prolific and inexhaustible in his creation of different ways to make a picture – which is just as well when you realise that *Vision On* ran for twelve series, *Take Hart* ran for eight and *Hart Beat* for ten. So proper rest and relaxation lay high in my parents' priorities.

Because of their frequent visits to Positano, they made friends in the town – one such being the Capraro family – Gennaro and his English wife Valerie and their children, Peter and Lara. Splitting their time between England and Italy, it was their son Peter who recognised my father from his television programmes as he was sauntering down the steps among the boutiques and galleries that led into the town. At eight years old Peter, with the unquestionable authority of the young, informed my father that he was Tony Hart and that he was not to move while he went to get the rest of his family. My father waited obediently and after a short while Gennaro arrived. He looked hard at Tony and then wagged his finger at him. 'I know you,' he said. A drink seemed to be in order, over which the Harts and the Capraros quickly bonded.

Subsequently my mother and father met up with the family every time they went to Positano. I met them for the first time a few years later when my husband Will and I were holidaying in Italy at the same time as my parents in a little village just up the coast from Positano. We had arranged to meet my parents and the Capraros in a restaurant down by the seashore, and I had elected to wear a short scarlet dress, Chinese in style with a mandarin collar and which fitted like a skin. In the restaurant Will and I were introduced to the rest of the Capraro family – to Gennaro who spoke heavily accented English, to Valerie who spoke Italian with a pronounced English accent, and to Peter and Lara, their bilingual children who switched effortlessly from one language to the other. Intent on giving us a proper Italian meal, Gennaro instructed the waiters at length on what to bring us. Over the course of the subsequent few hours, along with much wine, conversation and laughter, we ate garlic bread with antipasto – a mixed hors d'oeuvre that included salami, olives, marinated anchovies, ham, artichokes and peppers. Then we had pizza. Then we had rice balls and potato croquettes. Then we had fritti de mare – little fried fish, squid, whitebait and prawns. Then we had pasta; then meat. Eventually we finished up with a selection of glorious creamy Italian puddings, and I wished with all my heart that I had worn something with an elastic waistband.

Year after year, Tony and Jean went back to Positano to rest and recuperate after a gruelling season of devising and making television programmes. Although my father never worked on holiday, he would make a few sketches and take hundreds of photographs of rocks, flowers, steps, buildings, trees – anything that provided the inspiration to make pictures for his programmes. He and my mother would walk every day: up the mountain through the olive groves to Montepertuso or down the myriad steps that wound through the town to the beach, past whitewashed houses splashed with the vibrant colours of the flowers of the Mediterranean – bougainvillea, oleander and geraniums – sometimes venturing further afield, but not often. Then they would idle in the sun with their favourite books – Gerald Durrell, H E Bates, Ian Fleming or John Masters for Pa; Ed McBain, Patricia Wentworth or Agatha Christie for my mother – until it was time for a drink before dinner: a brandy and soda for him and a Campari for her. Every year, Positano worked its magic on their love life, which would sometimes flag a little under the pressure of Pa's work, and they would return home cuddling and kissing like a pair of newlyweds. And always they would return home with something for me – Italian liquorice in the early years, and garlic and olive oil for my kitchen later on.

The years went by, and their biannual visits to Positano continued, then, in 2002 just before Christmas, my mother had a stroke. Although weakened down one side, six weeks in hospital had her back on her feet again, and in a few more months she had improved still further. June approached and my father suggested that they should return to Italy, but my mother was uncertain, wondering if the trip would be too difficult. We talked, and I told her that although the journey would be hell, it would be worth it once she got there. She agreed and told Pa to contact Le Agavi, and off they went. They let British Airways know they required assistance – and by golly they got it. My mother was buggied through the terminal and lifted onto the aircraft at Gatwick; she was lifted out of it at Naples, wheel-chaired straight through the airport while her Italian porter airily waved her passport in the vague direction of the customs officials, popped into a taxi and whisked away to Positano. Once there, she swam every day, enjoyed the wonderful Italian food, ate, drank and laughed with the Capraros, made love with my father and revelled in the glorious Mediterranean sunshine for what – it later transpired – was to be the last time.

MY FATHER'S
GALLERY

The familiar theme tune 'Left Bank 2' plays as Tony presents the Gallery – an exhibition of work sent in by his young viewers. This he always introduces with a caption spelling out 'The Gallery', which he has formed from something relevant to the programme – tall thin letters which are illegible until viewed from a different angle; reflected writing; patchwork; prints. The ages of the young artists range from four to fourteen and are a rich mixture – scribbles, collages, detailed drawings, paintings and mosaics. Where materials have been stuck to the artwork, Tony lifts them slightly to show how the picture has been made or, over the music, he explains the technique a young artist has used to make their design.

For thirty years, young people sent their drawings in to my father's programmes in the hope that they would be shown. Over the years, different music has accompanied these young artists' pictures, but when *Vision On* began, it left indelibly in the minds of those who today are of a certain age the theme from the Gallery. Whenever this music is mentioned, it is almost always accompanied by the wail, 'I sent a picture in to the Gallery, but it was never shown!' My father neatly dealt with that one – 'Couldn't have been very good then, could it!'

Over the years, my father worked with a wealth of people, forming his own gallery of associates – many who exhibited brilliant talents of their own, and some of whom grew to become lifelong friends.

In the early sixties, Tony appeared alongside the ventriloquist Ray Alan in the children's television programme *Time for Tich*. Ray had made a trip to the BBC's Kensington House in West London to have a meeting with his producer, Leonard Chase, to talk about bringing new people with different talents into the series. My father, who had been visiting Kensington House on a totally different matter, chanced to walk past the open office door and waved to Leonard, whom he knew. Leonard called him in and introduced him to Ray who he knew by reputation but had not previously met. After a brief chat during which Ray told Pa what a wonderful artist he was, and Pa told Ray what a brilliant ventriloquist he was, Tony said that he ought to be going and started walking off down the corridor. Ray turned to his producer. 'What about him?' he suggested. Leonard chased after my father to call him back, and within minutes a deal was struck – *Time for Tich* was going to include an adventure story each week featuring Tich and Quackers to be illustrated by my father. And a new friendship was forged which was to last throughout my father's lifetime.

Although the production office was in Shepherd's Bush, the programme was made at the BBC's television studios in Manchester. Each week, Ray would arrive at our house to collect my father and they would fly up to Manchester together to make the programme which was soon re-titled *Tich and Quackers*. Ray always seemed to arrive when I (aged about five) would be having my tea, and generally wearing most of it across my face. 'It's Sticky Lips!' Ray would cry. 'Hallo little Sticky!' And Sticky I remained to Ray for almost 50 years until the end of his life. Having thus greeted me, he and my father would gather themselves together, bid my mother and I goodbye and go off down the garden path to the front gate. Ray would invariably link his arm through my father's, put the other hand on his hip and mince down the path saying loudly, 'Ooh, come on dearie or we'll be late.' I would find this hilariously funny, but my mother would say, 'Stop that – somebody might hear you and take you seriously!' because at that time, of course, homosexuality was a criminal offence.

While in Manchester, the pair of them would stay at a boarding house where the landlady, whose legs reputedly put an AA road map to shame on account of her varicose veins, ran an inexpensive but reasonably comfortable establishment. Her rules were rigid: in by 10pm or not at all, and no visitors in the bedrooms. My father she took to be a model guest, greeting him affectionately on one of his visits saying, 'Oh Mr 'Art, I've given your usual room to a young lady, so you're in number nine – I couldn't put her in number nine on account o' the mice.'

One evening, having gone out to dinner with some of the crew after recording *Tich and Quackers* (Ray having opted for an early night), my father didn't get back until after ten o'clock. In the true tradition of the northern British boarding house, the door was firmly locked and bolted and not a light shone anywhere. Tony tried throwing discreet handfuls of gravel at Ray's window, but to no avail. Disinclined to spend the night walking the streets of Manchester, he went to the local police station to ask if there was any chance of borrowing a cell for the night. The desk sergeant, although sympathetic, told Tony that he could only put him in a cell if he was destitute – had he got any money? My father turned out his pockets and found five pounds. 'I'm sorry sir,' said the sergeant, 'you're not destitute – you might try and find a hotel.' But by that time, all the hotels that could possibly have taken him in for a fiver were closed for the night, and the only place still open was a five-star establishment which did not have any rooms available for five pounds. So Tony walked the streets until 5am when he found himself outside the BBC just as the cleaning ladies were going in. He went in with them and took himself and his aching feet off to his dressing room for a couple of hours of rather uncomfortable shut-eye.

My father would arrive back home late at night two days later. Each week he and Ray would fly back down from Manchester to London and discuss what was going to be put into the programme the following week on the way. As the ideas came, my father would pull out one sick-bag after another from the pockets of the seats on the aircraft and rough out the next week's show. Once home, he would draw it all out in detail and the final script would be produced. It was fortunate that on those flights no one ever needed to use a sick-bag for the purpose for which it had been created – there were hardly ever any left! But my father did not forget me – it was the time of the Sindy doll, and while in Manchester he would shoot out to buy a new outfit for my Sindy and, when he got home, quietly creep into my room and slip it under my bed. In the morning, I would wake up, peek under the bed and find myself in a world of doll's clothes for the countryside, or swimming costumes or party frocks. I loved them.

At this time, my father's studio was one of the bedrooms in our house in Esher. It was the biggest bedroom, with double aspect windows, and ran from the front to the back of the house. Although I was not banned from the studio, I was not encouraged to go in whenever I felt like it, as it would disturb my father while he was working. He would, however, use me as a model from time to time. I remember being taken out of my bed at around nine o'clock one night when I was about five, put sleepily into a little vest and sat on the floor of the studio holding a bowl with the instruction to pretend to be eating rice from it with my fingers. My father had been asked to design a poster to be used as part of an appeal to raise money for starving children in Biafra. He didn't want to use the shocking images that are so familiar to us nowadays, but rather to suggest what could happen by using a healthy child as a model but drawing her much thinner than she actually was, with sunken eyes, and licking a finger after wiping it around an empty bowl.

On another occasion, he used me as a model in his book *The Young Letterer* – a book for children showing different ways of lettering. He had inked three fat black capital letters, A, B and C, on a clean white sheet of paper and wanted to photograph me apparently inking the letters myself. The camera was all set up; he dipped a brush into some ink and handed it to me saying, 'Just lay the brush on one of the letters as if you were doing it, and I'll take the picture.' I was absolutely terrified that I might drag the brush beyond the black ink and completely ruin his artwork – but all was well and I kept the brush within the confines of the letter. The studious result looked fine – and my look of deep concentration was brought about not by the careful drawing of the letters but by the fear of wrecking them.

Having the creative Tony Hart for a father certainly had its uses. From as far back as I can remember I always took part in the school Christmas play. In the first one, at about the age of six, I was cast as a soldier wearing black trousers with a red stripe down the sides and a red jacket with brass buttons. But I had no hat. A great bearskin would have been terrific, but difficult to make. So Pa came to the rescue and made for me a beautiful little red pillbox hat out of sticky-back textured paper with a strap made from black elastic held in place with paper fasteners. It wasn't until quite recently when I was looking at a photograph of two Queen's Gurkha officers in full dress uniform that I realised just where the style of my little pillbox hat had come from. On the second occasion, I was cast as Nokomis in *Hiawatha*. I had a maroon dress with a fringe and a black wig styled in two plaits. But I had no jewellery and the narrative referred to Nokomis's necklace made of 'wampum'. Again, Pa came to the rescue and my wampum necklace was created from uncooked macaroni painted in assorted colours with enamel paint and threaded on to a string. Very effective indeed.

While my father was making *Tich and Quackers*, my mother was also still working for the BBC, sometimes going away for days at a time filming on location for the detective drama series *Maigret* and later the police drama series *Z Cars*. This meant that over the years I had a string of au pairs looking after me. One of the earlier ones came from Switzerland; her name was Susie and her English wasn't particularly good. One day while my mother was away and I was having my afternoon nap, the telephone rang. My father was in the middle of laying down a watercolour wash on a huge sheet of paper on the studio floor and he had conscripted Susie to help him by holding the paper flat. 'Go and find out who it is,' he said, 'and tell them that I can't come to the phone as I am laying down a wash and you are helping me.' To his amusement, and some embarrassment, he heard Susie pick up the telephone and say in her heavily accented English, 'Meester 'Art cannot be disturbed. 'E is laying down to wash and I am 'elping 'im.'

The au pair girls changed quite frequently – hopefully because they only wanted to stay a short while in England and not because I was too much of a handful to look after – and some did cause a problem or two. A lovely girl from Norway lived with us for a while. She had a boyfriend who regularly came to the house, and sometimes both of them would take me out with them for tea, which was an enormous treat. But one day my mother came home to find the au pair lying on her bed curled up in agony. At first she wouldn't say what was wrong, but eventually she confessed that she had discovered she was pregnant and had gone to a backstreet abortionist who had treated her with some kind of spray. My mother immediately rang for our own doctor who came to the house and took care of the girl who, happily, was soon fit again. I, of course, was none the wiser of any of it.

Another au pair, a French girl, amused my parents hugely when she left us for the last time to return home. While in England, she had bought several three-quarter-length stiff petticoats that were the height of fashion at the time – enormous things which she could not squeeze into her suitcase. So she wore them home – all of them – and my mother said she looked wonderfully ridiculous as she walked down the garden path to the gate with her skirt and petticoats billowing up around her elbows.

All my au pair girls seemed to have their little quirks and foibles.

Above left: My father on a childhood holiday… perhaps with thoughts of gigantic drawings in the sand.

Above right: Sharing food with his 'brothers'. Tony, as St Francis, appears to be force-feeding Brother Juniper (played by Brian Davies).

Below: As Puck (front row, centre) in a production of Shakespeare's *A Midsummer Night's Dream*.

A new recruit, happy to be in India.

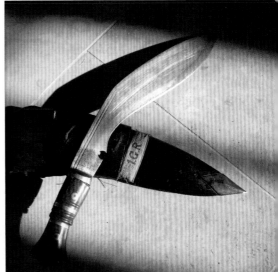

Above left: At the Indian Military Academy, Dehra Dun (front row).

Above right: My rather arty photo of Pa's 1st Gurkha Rifles regulation issue kukri.

Below: Pa kept in touch with his old regiment throughout his life. He is pictured here with Capt Shivakumar Limbu at our fund-raising do for the Gurkha Welfare Trust.

The artist as a young man, and Jean (*below left*) the young BBC secretary who captured his heart… permanently (*below right*).

Above: Christmas on the steps of the Hyde Park Hotel with Massara (far left), his wife Joan and their son Rooney. My mother has a fag on as usual.

Below: Watercolour, and pen and ink cartoon of the royal visit to the same hotel.

Above left: Pat Keysell signs for deaf viewers while Tony looks on.

Above right: Taking it on the chin for the sake of art. ©*BBC Archives*

Below: Ray, Tony and Quackers consider Tich's artistic ability – not bad for a dummy!

Above left: In the early years of marriage, outside Le Rondini.

Above right: The Hart family enthusiastically – but inelegantly – board a dinghy.

Below: A pen and wash sketch of the steps leading down to the rocks at Sori.

Above: A family lunch – setting the world to rights with wine and sunshine.

Below: The fairytale cottage in the heart of the Surrey countryside.

A Swedish girl would spend the evenings watching television while unconsciously picking at an embroidered cushion with her fingernails, eventually unpicking the entire design, much to my mother's irritation. It was this same girl that I got into terrible trouble. I would have been about seven. The garden fence was being repaired and the whole section that ran alongside a narrow alleyway that bordered the garden had been laid down flat on the grass. It was winter and my little friend Jackie from next door had come over to play while my au pair was setting her hair. Jackie and I played for a while in the garden and then thought it would be a great adventure to step across the fence and go by ourselves down the alley and across the green to the pond – naturally, without telling anybody. This we did and we played by the pond for a while. Then, it being almost Christmas, I had the enterprising notion of picking holly berries – the berries, mind you, not sprigs of holly which would have been much more useful – and going from door to door to see if we could sell them. Not surprisingly, nobody wanted to buy our handfuls of berries and, as it was dark, we thought it was probably time to go home. We made our way along the road that led to the alleyway, and as we started down the alley, I saw my father silhouetted against a street lamp holding a torch and walking towards us. Instead of giving us the cheerful greeting I anticipated, his face was set and grim. As he drew level with us, he did not shout and yell, demanding to know where we'd been, but simply said, tight-lipped, 'Come with me. You're late for Jackie's father's birthday.' In silence he escorted us to the flat where Jackie lived and where we had all been invited for a party. Needless to say, it was not a very merry occasion. Although we didn't realise it, we had been missing for about three hours. I remember sitting beside Jackie on the sofa nursing a glass of something sweet and fizzy in almost total silence. My poor au pair was in a state of nervous collapse thinking she had lost her charge and both Jackie's and my parents had been beside themselves with worry imagining us to be dead or kidnapped, or both. However, we were not in disgrace for very long and although Pa was angry with me, he was far angrier with the au pair, who should have been keeping an eye on us – although we of course should have known better than to wander off by ourselves without letting anybody know where we were going. But you don't think of that when you're seven.

My poor Pa had a similar worry thinking he had lost his child on another occasion only a short time later. There were letters to post, and I begged him to let me go by myself to the postbox on the corner to post them. Reluctantly he agreed, on the condition that I ran to the letter box, posted the letters and then ran straight back – being very careful when crossing the road. I agreed to this, and went off clutching the letters. I stopped at the road, and crossed it carefully, and then went to the postbox and posted the letters. Stopping at the road again, I saw my mother behind the wheel of our car turning into the very road I was crossing. She stopped and asked if I wanted to ride with her to the shops. Of course I did, so I jumped in beside her. We went to the local grocer's shop and got some bits and pieces, stopping to chat for a while with the grocer, and then climbed back into the car and drove home. This time, it was my father who was having a nervous breakdown as I had been gone much too long and he was convinced I was lost, murdered or kidnapped. And this time it was my mother who bore the brunt of his wrath.

The last au pair to live with us before I went off to boarding school was an Irish girl called Sylvia. She was lovely with no obvious idiosyncrasies. She adored my parents and was fond of me, but she had a phobia about any kind of insect. Tucking me into bed one night, she watched in puzzlement as I carefully lifted my pillow and turned it over. I explained that this was a ritual I performed every night to make sure that there were no spiders under my pillow – and of course there never were. Later that night as Sylvia got into bed she decided to check under her own pillow, and there to her horror, crouched on the sheet, was an enormous, big-bodied hairy spider. Sylvia's hysterical screams had both my mother and father rushing to her room convinced she was being torn limb from limb by an intruder.

Pa was an adept at dealing with spiders, no matter how big they were. He would simply catch them softly in his hand and drop them outside into the nearest flowerbed, saying with a gentle admonishment to his terrified womenfolk, 'They won't hurt you, you know.' Always wanting to emulate my father, I could deal with spiders in the same way – but only up to a certain size. I picked up my last big spider when I was 18. My grandmother was staying with us, and my mother and I had been turning out the contents of the priest-hole – an access into the loft area of the cottage reached via a small door halfway up the wall of my parents' bedroom. We had pulled down a load of stuff from the loft onto the bed when a colossal spider strolled out and over the bedcover. My grandmother shrieked and retreated to the corner of the room, while my mother regarded the gigantic arachnid with a modicum of alarm. 'Leave it to me!' I cried heroically. 'Somebody open a window.' My mother opened the window and I picked up the spider, which I could swear was as big as a mouse. Walking calmly to the open window, I could feel it moving about inside my cupped hands, its legs tickling my palms and its big body bumping against them. Maintaining an air of dignified composure, I reached the window and threw it out – and then completely wrecked my calm show of bravery by frantically brushing the palms of my hands together and leaping around the room, shivering uncontrollably and shouting, 'Yuck! Yuck! Yuck!' for some minutes. These days, I deal with the big ones with the help of a glass and a magazine.

But it wasn't just spiders that terrified Sylvia. In summer, we would often have our lunch outside sitting at a table under the walnut tree, which would periodically drop seed pods that looked exactly like caterpillars. Our peaceful lunches in the garden would be punctuated by Sylvia's screams as she leapt out of her chair flapping wildly but ineffectually at herself as the 'caterpillars' dropped onto her head and shoulders.

The walnut tree in question was a splendid specimen with high, broad branches that cast a cool shade over the garden. The bark of its trunk was so furrowed that I could almost find handholds and footholds in it to climb up, but not quite. But our dog, the wire-haired terrier whose correct name was Sherry, but who had always been known as Baggy ever since she had rapidly but temporarily lost a lot of weight, could get her little paws into the spaces in the bark and scramble high up the trunk to where it forked into the first branches. She could not, however, get down. Inside the house, the family would become dimly aware that barking had been going on for some considerable time, and one of us would wander out to see what was going on. There she would stand, precariously balanced on a large knot, high up in the walnut tree, desperately barking for help. My father would chuckle, and taking a run at the trunk of the tree, would swarm up it until he reached the stuck dog. Relieved to be rescued, Baggy would allow herself to be placed on my father's shoulders and carried back down the tree to safety. It doesn't say much for her doggy memory that this was a process that was frequently repeated.

This dog of ours had many little quirks and foibles. She was not a slim animal, and as she grew older she grew rounder. She would sit for ages on her fat little rump by the side of our chairs as we sat with guests at meal times, embarrassingly begging for food. My grandmother – this was my mother's mother, who had taken part in the giant spider episode – doted on the dog, and for some reason took it into her head that all cats were female and all dogs were male. One hot summer afternoon Baggy, who was even rounder than usual due to being heavily and obviously pregnant, toiled up the garden path panting as she went towards my grandmother, who was standing at the open front door. My father was delighted by her sympathetic if somewhat inaccurate remark: 'Poor little man!' she said.

My father would describe Baggy as mainly white with a couple of black and brown patches, one ear that stuck straight up, one that flopped over, four legs – and an anecdote. 'Why an anecdote?' I asked him. Ever one to enjoy a play on words he replied, 'Because an anecdote is a short funny tale!' Baggy joined the Hart family at the same time as I did, so we grew up together until she sloughed off her mortal coil when we were both 14. Due to her whiteness and her fondness for grubby places, she was quite a difficult dog to keep clean and would have to submit to a bath on a fairly frequent basis. First, my old plastic baby bath would be placed in the big tub and warm water added. Then Baggy would be found and her collar removed. At this, the dog would start to shake and look utterly dejected whereupon she would be scooped up and carried bodily up the stairs into the bathroom and plonked into her bath. There she would sit, trembling from head to paw while we shampooed her with doggy shampoo – paying great attention to her nether regions, which were always a bit mucky, and of course to her 'anecdote'. Then she would be rinsed and lifted out of the bath. This was always the tricky part of the operation because all she wanted to do was make an instant bid for freedom, but we needed to get her as dry as possible first in order to save the furniture and the carpets. With my mother holding Baggy firmly wrapped in one towel, my father tried to dry any protruding parts of dog with another, saying, 'Hold her! Hold her!' while Baggy wriggled furiously until she inevitably managed to escape from my mother's grip. Then she would fly out of the bathroom like a bat out of hell, gallop down the stairs and into the sitting room where, nose first, she would tear along the sides of the settees and chairs, rubbing herself as she went. This would be followed by what looked like some kind of doggy break-dancing as she lay on the carpet on her side and scooted herself rapidly round in circles snuffling and grunting. Finally, she would shoot out of the house to find a patch of dust to roll in until she had got herself back to her own nice, familiar off-white colour again.

Lost children, errant au pairs and dogs aside, my father continued to travel to Manchester with Ray each week. *Tich and Quackers* had become established as a children's entertainment show and featured Tich, a cheeky schoolboy dummy clad in school cap and blazer, and Quackers, a very cute white and fluffy puppet duck. Also featured each week was a pop group or solo singer, and an animal which Tony would borrow from Bellevue Zoo to talk about and sketch on the programme. Tich, through Ray, spoke volumes of nonsense, generally rude, while Quackers could only quack. This charming, fluffy character was operated by none other than my father who would be crouched behind Ray's desk with a duck-call whistle in his mouth and one arm in the air with its hand up a duck.

The solo singer one week was Lulu who, having sung her song, came over to the desk to talk to Ray and Tich and Quackers. Everyone loved Quackers, and Lulu was no exception. Ray introduced her to Tich, who was his usual cheeky self, and then to Quackers. Lulu immediately put her arms around the duck and clasped him lovingly to her bosom, murmuring words of endearment, completely forgetting that she was actually cuddling my father's hand clad in a duck costume. Tony (and Quackers) promptly froze, at which point Lulu suddenly realised what she was doing, and released Quackers with alacrity.

During the making of this series, Bellevue Zoo had promised my father a female skunk to show on the programme, but when he went to collect it, he was told that she couldn't be taken out because she was pregnant. The zookeeper said this was no problem and that my father could have a male skunk instead. 'He's been neutered,' said the keeper. 'He won't make a smell.' So my father bore the male skunk away, hoping that the keeper was right. In the studio shortly afterwards, everything was going swimmingly and they were rehearsing the animal spot, which was to be followed by a number from the sixties pop group The Swinging Blue Jeans, who were standing ready in position. The skunk looked lovely, but as Tony was moving it about to show the marvellous black-and-white stripes, suddenly the animal did what it shouldn't have been able to do – it made the most appalling smell. The aroma caught my father by the throat. Eyes streaming, coughing and choking, Tony tried to speak but could only make strange strangled noises. The director flipped the speaker switch so that he could be heard on the studio floor and told my father to stop mucking about. Tony tried to reply, but could only manage a series of wheezing grunts. 'I'm coming down!' yelled the director angrily, and made his way furiously to the floor. He was halfway across it when the smell attacked him. He stopped dead in his tracks and produced a series of similar strange choking sounds. The pop group and the studio personnel were evacuated, fans were switched on and the big dock doors were opened wide to let in the fresh air. Eventually the smell began to die away and artistes and crew were able to go back and pick up where they had left off to complete the programme; it all went off without a hitch.

It was a week later when Tony saw the long-haired denim-clad pop group in the canteen. He went over to them and, with a happy smile, apologised for the awful smell in the studio the week before. The group just looked at him. 'It was the skunk,' he explained, 'it should have been a female, but it wasn't.' The group continued to look at him as if he had come from another planet. Puzzled, Tony went back to his team and said, 'It's very odd, but they don't seem to remember the skunk and the terrible smell in the studio last week.' One of them patted his hand. 'That's because they were the Swinging Blue Jeans. Those guys over there are the Rolling Stones.'

Tich and Quackers began in 1963, and on Christmas day of that year, and for many subsequent Christmases, my father and Ray Alan took part in a live programme on Christmas morning that was presented by Leslie Crowther and broadcast from Queen Mary's Children's Hospital at Carshalton in Surrey. It was a heart-warming entertainment show featuring Ray and his ventriloquist act with Tich and Quackers, and Tony doing his drawing, all held together with jokes from Leslie Crowther, who would wear a wire coat hanger on his head. This would have a piece of mistletoe hanging from it over his forehead, giving him the excuse to kiss every nurse in sight. The show was transmitted live from the children's bedsides and they adored it. For Ray's section of the show, he would sit beside one of the sick children making Tich talk, and my father would be lying on his back under the child's bed with his arm in the air working Quackers.

They rehearsed the show on Christmas Eve, and one year I went with them. I sat with those children from other wards who were well enough to be dressed and out of bed for a little while, and watched in fascination as Leslie Crowther undid his trousers in order to feed the microphone wire down his trouser leg and along the floor – no radio mikes in those days. The rehearsal went well, and when it was over the children were rounded up ready to be taken back to their respective wards. The matron in charge came across to me saying, 'Which ward are you in, dear?' I told her that I wasn't in a ward but was with my father. 'Who is your father, dear?' she asked. 'Tony Hart,' I replied proudly. 'Now don't be silly dear,' she said. 'Which ward are you in?' For a moment I was terrified that I was going to be bundled off into some anonymous ward and lost forever, but thankfully at that moment my father came across and asked me if I was ready to go.

Because the programme was broadcast live on Christmas Day, lunch was always held back until Pa got home, which would be at around two o'clock, and presents were not opened until after lunch – instigating a tradition that was upheld throughout my parents' lifetime, and continues in our family to this day.

As time went on, Tony was to make frequent guest appearances on other people's shows – one of them being *The Generation Game*, where he appeared several times on the show hosted by Larry Grayson and later Jim Davidson. This show, some of you may remember, involved two teams consisting of Mum and Dad and a brace of grown-up offspring being shown how to do something, and then doing it themselves – and of course the worse they performed, the better viewing it made. Tony would demonstrate a way of making a picture on a huge sheet of paper placed on the floor, on which prints were made using rollers, blocks, bits of wood, hands and feet – and the messier it got, the better it looked. For his appearance on Jim Davidson's show he showed the contestants how to make a picture of a dragon using a pre-formed teardrop shape dipped in green paint printed several times on paper, to give the shape of the creature, and then adding white and red prints to give teeth, claws and a flaming tongue. The contestants then had a go, some producing a reasonable picture, others producing a hilarious beast too long in the leg, too short in the neck, and looking like something cuddly you might want to take home with you.

When Pa appeared on *The Generation Game* with Larry Grayson, he had been instructed by the production team to bring something with him to chat with Larry about before getting on with the artwork. Along with his catchphrase of 'Shut that door' Larry had a friend of whom he often spoke but who we never saw, called Slack Alice – and my father hit upon the perfect thing to bring: a fan of

Alice in Wonderland since childhood, my father was struck by the similarity Larry Grayson bore to the Mad Hatter, and the reference to Slack Alice made it perfect. Tony tried to tell Larry about what he was going to show him before they started recording the programme, but Larry backed away crying, 'Don't show me, don't show me! Wait until we're recording!' He wanted a spontaneous reaction, so my father waited, and when he was introduced, Larry said, 'Show us what you've brought!' Whatever he was expecting, it certainly wasn't an illustration from *Alice in Wonderland*, and Larry was rendered momentarily and uncharacteristically speechless as my father compared him to the Mad Hatter, and pointed out that Alice, leaning back in her chair at the tea party, really did look remarkably slack.

It was another from my father's gallery of friends and admirers in the world of television who presented him with his BAFTA Lifetime Achievement award in 1998 – Neil Buchanan. Having grown up watching my father, Neil went on to present *Art Attack*, his own art programme for children, and was thrilled when they met for the first time when they were both involved in a BBC Red Nose Day – the annual culmination of fund-raising events for Comic Relief. With both TV artists sporting a plastic red nose and looking very silly, Neil made a big artwork using red nose tomatoes which were the theme for that year, while my father created some delightful red nose tomato characters – afterwards drawing one for Neil's daughter, which hangs in the Buchanan home to this day. Neil, who presented ITV's *Art Attack* from 1989 to 2007, shares the widespread conviction that my father paved the way for the genre of children's art on television in the days when children's television was, as he put it, wholesome, inspiring and empowering. He felt that *Art Attack* survived partly because it did battle in the big bad world of ratings wars and commercially led decision making, but principally because it was built very firmly on those same values and standards as my father's shows. In a letter to me Neil added, 'The thing I have carried with me through the years from those inspirational shows is the way he communicated with ME. On a one-to-one basis Tony Hart was communicating with me. Just me! He was in my living room teaching me how to draw. He was always real. Just him ... and me the viewer ... in my lounge. Brilliant!'

UPS AND DOWNS

Looking down on a smooth sandy beach with the tide out, we see Tony striding out manfully with a rake. Rapidly, using the rake as a tool, he draws a long, horizontal line in the sand. Then he makes several huge curves and, with a final sweep and a swirl, a vast elephant is revealed. Tony walks across the sand, following his drawn line, and makes a smaller picture at the other end with his rake; this time it's a mouse. Viewed from on high, and by tilting the camera to the right and the left, we see the elephant and the mouse seated at either end of a seesaw which is swinging up and down.

All of us experience good and bad things that happen in our lives – and without the bad, we wouldn't appreciate the good. My father's life was filled with mostly good things – the love of his family, a brilliant talent, a beautiful home and, although not straightaway, just the right amount of fame.

Although my father had been working in television for more than ten years, it wasn't until 1964 and the start of *Vision On* that he became well-known. And one of the most popular items that he presented was the exhibition of viewers artwork - The Gallery. The thousands of pictures – sometimes 10,000 in a week – that were sent in to the programme were first scrutinized by a small workforce of retired ladies and gentlemen who would discard the majority, and Tony would be given a much reduced number of pictures to choose from. My father liked to imagine these people starting the day with enormous enthusiasm, showing each other the pictures made by the young viewers and saying, 'Ah, Bert, come and look at this, isn't that good?' and then by the end of the day viciously sorting the pictures into rapid piles and saying, 'No. No. Yes. No. Maybe. No,' and so on. Pa would reduce the number to around 50, and then he and producer Patrick Dowling would make the final choice of 24 to appear in the Gallery –

trying to show at least two pictures representative of each age, from four to fourteen.

The programme format included not only picture-making, but a great deal of humour and comedy. There was Grog, the *Vision On* logo designed by my father, which wrote itself, turned itself on its end, then printed a mirror image of itself. Looking very much like some sort of oriental grasshopper, it then bounced itself out of the picture. My father's first co-presenters were Pat Keysell and Ben Benison, later followed by Wilfred Makepeace Lunn and Sylvester McCoy, plus many animated things –including a delightfully dim animated dinosaur by the name of Auggie and a long fluffy orange thing on a wire called the Woofumpuss, which whizzed around making a racket. Captioned conversations were held between the Burbles – two invisible somethings that lived in a grandfather clock and conversed in speech bubbles – and between Humphrey and Susanne, a young girl and a tortoise.

Although the programme was designed specifically for deaf children, it appealed to everybody else – and it had a wonderful wackiness about it which, looking at it today, has withstood the test of time. Pat Keysell presented the programme using both normal speech and sign language. 'We are sorry we cannot return your drawings, but there is a prize for any that we show' – remember? Each programme would have a theme – Coils and Springs, Signs and Signals, Triangles, Waves and Opposites, to name but a few – and everything in it would have some relevance to that theme. In a programme with a theme of 'Light', my father was seen running up and down the stairs of a high-rise office block switching lights on and off as he went. A long shot of the building after he had finished revealed the figure of a rampant lion created from an illuminated mosaic from the lighted windows. Another programme with the theme of 'Stone' had Ben Benison, a mime artist, providing the comedy by spending a great deal of time with back braced and knees bent heaving an enormous lump of invisible rock about. Eventually he staggered with it out through a door in the set leading on to a landing – there was a splintering crash and a cutaway shot of Pat watching him with a look of alarm – and then a cut back to the landing, now with totally wrecked banisters and no sign of Ben.

Director Clive Doig explained that because of the minimal use of speech, *Vision On* appealed not only to the deaf and partially deaf, but also to the old, the young, and those of other nationalities – the programme was truly universal. As we've already seen, the show made frequent use of the combination of art and comedy. Filming outside on a ski slope in Switzerland, using a roller and sponges dipped into trays of coloured paint, my father created a giant scene on paper of skiers whizzing down a snowy mountain, and then, when the picture was finished, two skiers came whizzing down the mountain and – circus-style – jumped through the paper, turning the picture into real life. Similarly, a drawing of a huge whale spurted real water through its blow-hole into my father's face as he leaned in to the picture to finish it off.

Vision On spawned an enormous amount of talent, including two young animation film-makers named David Sproxton and Peter Lord. They produced short animated cartoon inserts for the programme featuring a superhero called Aardman who lacked superpowers but did wear his pants outside his trousers. Having completed their first animated film they needed to be paid, and as Peter and David had not yet formed a company and a cheque needed to be written, they had to decide on a name for their business quickly – so they used their character's name and called themselves Aardman Animations. Their legendary company, born in the kitchen of a flat in Bristol, now occupies two vast sites in that same city and has gone on to do great things, including the production of the award-winning *Creature Comforts* and *Wallace & Gromit* animated films; feature-length films including *Chicken Run* and *Wallace & Gromit: Curse of the Were-Rabbit*; and the first of their CGI productions – *Flushed Away*. Now world class and world famous, Aardman continues to flourish, making feature films, commercials, children's programmes and TV shorts.

Another item in *Vision On* was The Prof in the shape of David Cleveland. In these short speeded-up film items, the Prof was featured getting into ridiculous scrapes, sometimes involving other characters which were also played by himself. One adventure had him cycling in the countryside when he was accosted by a burglar – immediately recognisable by his stripy jumper and the mask over his eyes. The Prof and burglar chased each other around a tree for a moment – one always disappearing behind the branches before the other appeared – then the burglar broke away, ran to the bicycle and attempted to ride it away but went round and round in tight circles and fell over. As the Prof ran towards him, the burglar fled, hurling himself over a fence and running away across a field. The Prof wheeled the bicycle to the fence and then hurled himself over it and followed the burglar, and then, thanks to the magic of stop-frame animation, the bicycle chucked itself over the fence and followed after them. All this was speeded up on film and accompanied by comic music; it was absolutely hilarious – and also innovative in that this type of real-life stop-frame animation had not been seen on the television screen before.

My father would interact with Pat and Ben, but his main purpose was to make pictures relevant to the theme of the programme and he would use anything – clay, sand, ink, stone, string – to make his designs. He would make impressions in a piece of flat clay or Plasticine, using nuts, bolts, cogs, wheels and skewers – anything that made an interesting shape. Then, using a small roller, he would roll some water-based ink over the clay – just as one would for a lino cut. Next, he would take a piece of paper, press it down over the inked clay, and using his hands as a press, take an impression. The ink would leave a textured effect, and the cogs and wheels and skewer shapes would be reversed out of the textured background to create an abstract picture. This would be mounted on the wall in a frame to show it off to its best effect. Sometimes, my father's designs would be more of a model than a picture. For a programme with the theme of 'Stone', he simply took a mirror, laid it flat and poured sand all around the edge of it, then placed a few pieces of rock onto the sand. With a change of camera angle and lighting, it became a lagoon landscape.

Another regular item on the programme was the picture that drew itself. My father would be drawing this back-to-front on paper placed over glass, which was reflected in a mirror. By filming the mirror image with clever positioning of the camera and subtle lighting in the quiet, darkened studio, the picture appeared to draw itself.

One of the essential characteristics of *Vision On* was the music that accompanied the items and provided such contrast – the comic staccato music that accompanied The Prof, John Williams's reflective guitar piece *Cavatina* which went with the pictures that drew themselves, and of course the familiar notes of *Left Bank 2* – the theme that accompanied the Gallery. For so many children, the Gallery was the high spot of the programme – would the picture they had laboured over be chosen to appear? And after a week of waiting, can you imagine the cheers of delight at home when the young artist's masterpiece appeared on the screen, captioned with their name and age. *Vision On's* gallery of viewer's artwork was among the first instances of interactive children's television, lending hugely to its popularity, and it has formed part of not just my father's programmes, but also more recent programmes such as *SMart* and *Art Attack*.

Another engaging aspect of my father's picture making was that he never insisted on a slavish copy of what he was doing but would constantly invite the viewers to use their own imaginations, to use different colours or shapes or objects. He would show how a picture could be made, suggesting at the same time how it could be varied. He would take the most enormous delight in seeing how the young viewers had taken the ideas that he had demonstrated in their submissions for the Gallery, and made them their own.

Vision On grew out of a rather more staid programme that had been running since 1952 with the imaginative title *For Deaf Children*, which was intended purely for children who were hard of hearing. With *Vision On*'s introduction of animation, mime, comic film and my father's inventive picture-making, the programme rapidly became popular not only with both deaf and hearing children, but also with viewers all over the world – appearing in 60 countries – and in 1972 was the first BBC children's series to be sold to the United States. The programme's producer, Patrick Dowling, said in an interview with Joan Bakewell for the *Radio Times* in 1976, 'Deaf children are just like others except they can't hear, so we made a programme that wouldn't matter whether you were deaf or not.' Joan Bakewell herself added that it proved too that grown-ups didn't need to be confined to an adult ghetto. She found *Vision On* to be one of the most upbeat, original and refreshing things on television, and that much of the credit for that lay with my father. She went on to describe him as: 'Tony Hart, the programme's central presenter and conceiver of a million things to do with string, wire, paint, cardboard and imagination.'

Although Patrick Dowling was a most visionary producer, constantly breaking new ground with *Vision On*, my father's relationship with him was not an easy one. My father would test and practise the pictures he was going to make for his programmes over and over again, needing to be properly prepared and totally in control. Patrick would push Pa, looking for a new angle, a new edge on what he was doing, and would ask him at the last minute to change what had been rehearsed. My father never said 'No', but sometimes the energy would drain from him and he would sink into a trough of despair. Meetings to discuss the programmes would be difficult, too. Pa would drive up to Television Centre in west London promptly on time for a ten o'clock meeting with Patrick and director Christopher Pilkington. Christopher would be there, but Patrick would on occasion not turn up until later, whereupon he would sometimes metaphorically rip to shreds everything that Christopher and my father had decided upon while they were waiting. But, difficult or not, *Vision On* with Patrick Dowling at the helm received worldwide acclaim, winning in 1970 BAFTA's Harlequin Award for Children's Programmes, in 1972 the Prix Jeunesse – a worldwide award for children's television, and in 1973 a BAFTA for Specialised Series – the first time a children's programme appeared in this category.

Two years after the start of *Vision On*, we moved from our suburban house in Esher to a half-timbered Elizabethan cottage in the depths of the Surrey countryside, which is a mile away from the nearest shop and is where my father lived up until his death in 2009. This beautiful little cottage still nestles in a large garden full of flowers, with lawns on two levels, pear trees and apple trees jostling each other for space and hops rambling over the hedges. But my mother, who had already been having some doubts about the move, thought perhaps they were making a terrible mistake, as it was comparatively isolated and a long way from their friends in Esher. My father had told me all about it, describing the waterfall that you could hear and just see from what was going to be my bedroom window, the priest-hole in their bedroom, and the fireplace that you could sit in. This all sounded like something out of a fairy tale but had me completely puzzled, as I couldn't work out how it was possible to sit in a fireplace and not get burned – until I saw and understood what an inglenook fireplace was.

Just before we moved, at a time when my father was away filming, my mother set pen to paper in a letter to him saying:

'I sometimes think you and I are some kind of masochists – we get comfortably settled down and then disrupt everything by getting restless – perhaps it's a kind of guilt complex – life becomes so easy we have to make it difficult for ourselves again. At least it keeps us aware and alive! I'm eager for a change until it actually happens, then I go all peculiar and weepy and a crashing bore to all and sundry, and most especially to you my darling.'

But my parents rapidly grew to love their country cottage with a passion, and adapted it over the years to suit their purposes. Indeed, from time to time over the 36 years that they lived there together, they would go and look at other houses thinking that perhaps they ought to move – but could never find anywhere that they liked as much as where they already were. The garden is where Tony had his greatest influence. The house faced north, and when we arrived there was a bit of hard-standing outside the kitchen door to the east, and a small patio to the west. Very quickly, my father built a pond beyond the west patio, complete with a waterfall, water lilies, goldfish and periodic newts and frogs. Later, he put some stone down behind the house, creating a sheltered terrace to the south with a passionflower climbing all over the wall. Lastly, he created a sunken terrace at the front of the house, which is reached by a couple of steps down through bushes and rockeries and is shaded by apple and pear trees. I remember one wonderful weekend in the early years of my first marriage when we followed the sun round the house all day, moving from terrace to terrace for lunch, then tea, then supper.

Ever the gourmand, my father conceived a plan to use part of the garden to farm snails, a delicacy of which he was particularly fond when cooked with garlic, parsley, shallots and butter. He travelled up to London to Harrods with the happy assumption that they would be able to supply him with a quantity of live, edible breeding snails – the store then having the reputation for being able to supply anything. Alas, the world-famous Knightsbridge store was unable to comply with this request but, undaunted, my father returned home laden with several tins of snails and some earthenware snail dishes to cook them in. A keen and talented cook, my father would experiment with all manner of ingredients, and with his artist's eye for form and shape would revel in producing dishes that needed to be moulded and turned out. He particularly enjoyed making game terrine – packed with local rabbit, pheasant, duck and lead shot that you had to be careful not to break your teeth on – and his egg mousse, which on a first tasting I had lied and said I liked. This was to be a salutary lesson in not lying, even when it seems to be the right thing to do, because on many a visit to the cottage in later years, my darling dad would produce his egg mousse by way of a starter, saying with a smile, 'I know you like it!' I never had the heart to confess that I didn't, and would eat it up with apparent relish. However, he treated me in much the same way. Finding ourselves on our own one lunchtime when I was about ten, I volunteered to make lunch for us, a gourmet meal of fishfingers and baked beans. After spending some time and effort in the kitchen, I summoned him from his studio and sat him down at the kitchen table where he dutifully munched his way through fishfingers that were still frozen in the middle and baked beans that were burned. I reckon we're square.

My father could be described as having a charmed existence – he was successful in his work, happy at home and blessed with a wonderful wife, a delightful dog and me, and he rarely seemed to come into contact with the darker side of life. There was one occasion, however, when driving home one evening after a few busy studio days in Bristol, he pulled over to pick up a hitchhiker. The man got into the car and thanked Pa for stopping. They made pleasant small talk for a few miles and then the tone of the conversation changed. 'Nice car this,' said the man. My father agreed that it was. 'Do alright for yourself, don't you?' Pa cautiously said that he was very fortunate. Suddenly it all began to get very unpleasant with the hitchhiker saying that it was unfair that people like my father had everything while he had nothing. Then when he started calling my father all sorts of horrible names and demanding money, Pa knew he had to get him out of the car as quickly as possible. Coolly he assessed the situation and, being aware that he knew exactly what the car was going to do and his passenger didn't, my father suddenly wrenched the steering wheel hard over and swerved into the side of the road. Screeching to an abrupt stop he reached across the man and flung open the passenger door. 'Get out!' he snapped. Stunned by the sudden manoeuvre and Pa's authoritative attitude, the hitchhiker meekly got out of the car and loped off into the darkness. Upset by the experience, and angry that someone who he had been trying to help should behave in this way, my father drove home to my mother and the peace and tranquillity of their country cottage.

Both of my parents took a delight in adapting the cottage to suit their needs. A purpose-built studio with lots of light was built in the garden, ten steps away from the back door, outside of which hung a bell. Whenever a meal was ready, my mother would lean out of the kitchen door to ring the bell to summon my father and he, responding like one of Pavlov's dogs, would answer the summons and trot into the kitchen, drooling gently. The kitchen was extended and fitted with oak cupboards, an Italian tiled floor and – to my mother's total delight – an eye-level double oven. A room to hold all their books was added to the back of the cottage, and additional windows to let in more light were put in the drawing room and the bathroom. The bathroom window was particularly effective, since it ran along the entire length of the bath – although this was not the original intention. A medium-sized window was going to be positioned alongside the bath, and this was measured inside and out respectively by two of the builders, Brian and Henry. Then came the task of knocking out the wall, Henry working on the inside and Brian working on the outside. After the plaster had been pulled away from the inside and the brickwork loosened on the outside, Brian called to Henry to break through. With a great smashing and banging, Henry broke through the bathroom wall to find that he had placed his window to align with the top end of the bath, and Brian's window had been envisaged at the bottom end. Undaunted, my parents settled for a long window running the length of the bath, which for the rest of their days rejoiced in the name of 'Henry's Hole'.

Henry's Hole featured in one of the Sunday magazines. My father having said that his favourite form of relaxation after a busy day was to have a brandy and soda in the bath, the magazine decided to photograph him in it. The photographer and several others descended on the cottage and all crowded into the bathroom, where a bath full of bubbles was run for him. It all took quite a time to set up and eventually, modestly clad in a pair of swimming trunks, Pa pushed his way through the throng and climbed into the bath clutching his brandy and soda. Looking through his viewfinder, the photographer announced, 'I can see the swimming trunks', so one of the magazine people swished the water around with a limp hand in an attempt to generate more bubbles. 'No, I can still see them,' said the photographer. Unwilling to spend any more time than was absolutely necessary in the bath with someone swishing the water around in an area just a little too close for comfort, Pa jumped out muttering, 'Oh for goodness' sake!' and pulled off his trunks in front of his interested audience before leaping back into the tepid water. He seized his glass and, stitching a broad smile on his face, raised it to the photographer. The picture is good – but to those of us who know him well, there is definitely some irritation to be seen behind the smile.

When he wasn't being photographed in the bathroom, my father enjoyed nothing more than a deep, blazing hot bath, usually scented with either a pine essence, which coloured the water a deep green, or a few drops of Floris. He would generally have his bath at around six o'clock in the evening, and due to its heat and depth, I loved jumping into it after he had finished. One evening, when I had just returned home from school for the holidays and Pa was on his way upstairs to his bath, I called up to him, 'Can I have it after you?'

'Course,' said Pa as he continued up the stairs, adding as an afterthought, 'I won't pee in it.' Then he stopped and looked back down at me with a grin. 'On second thoughts, if you're having it after me, I *will* pee in it!' He was joking, of course. At least I hope he was!

My father drew his inspiration from every room in the house – the bathroom wallpaper was an inspiration in its own right, the green and yellow design seeming to be made up of small plant-like creatures holding their arms up in a kind of Gallic shrug. I watched the creation of a way of making an interesting design evolve over lunch in the kitchen one day. We were eating spaghetti with a tomato and garlic sauce that my mother had made – a big favourite at home. My father had eaten about half his food when, with his fork, he dragged a looped strand of spaghetti through the sauce on his plate. He did it again, then picked up his plate and with a muttered 'Excuse me' went out to his studio. My mother and I raised our eyebrows at each other and carried on with our lunch.

By the end of the afternoon, the plate-and-spaghetti experiment had evolved into a fabulous textured wave-like design. My father had created this by dipping pieces of string into coloured paint and laying them in coils and curves on a piece of card – making sure to leave the two ends free. He then placed another piece of card over the top and holding it down, dragged the string out from between the two pieces of paper, at the same time creating an abstract design of waves and curves.

It is quite likely that the plate never found its way back to the kitchen – it was a constant source of mild annoyance to my mother that all sorts of promising kitchen utensils – forks (good for printing a grass effect), egg whisks (bubbling up paint to take a print off the surface perhaps?), meat hooks (printing again), a potato masher (for spraying paint through to achieve a chequered effect) and a cheese grater (goodness knows what he did with that!) – would vanish into the studio to play their part in the creation of yet another stunning artwork.

Many of my father's ideas for creating a design came about by accident. He spilt some black powder paint onto the formica table in his studio one day, and tried to get if off with washing-up liquid and a scrubbing brush. Realising that he was making the most marvellous toothcomb textures, he repeated the black powder paint spillage onto a piece of card, mixed it with some washing-up liquid and then cut out a cardboard comb. Drawing the comb through the ink mixture, he created a fantastic swirling ribbon design.

Trotting out to Pa's studio with tea or a message, I encountered many weird and wonderful things that a child wouldn't generally come across when visiting their father's place of work: green sponge forests scattered over the scale model of a papier-mâché landscape with a blue-ink pool lying in the deepest section of a valley; a series of circular patterns created by a cone full of salt swinging on a long string above a sheet of black paper laid out on the floor; blown eggs painted in different colours with little faces, peeping at me from all corners of the studio. All manner of extraordinary things that to me were simply part of my father's normal working day. Sometimes I would go and sit quietly at the table in his studio while he worked, rarely making designs from the enormous variety of materials available but content just to draw for hours, in a companionable silence, with a pencil or felt-tip pen on the back of his old scripts.

By this time, I was at a boarding school. I was eight years old, and the journey from our home to the school in Brighton took about an hour and a half. My heart would sink as we passed the Devil's Dyke, and a dark cloud of misery would envelop me. On my very first day we pulled up outside the boarding house and my father turned round from the driving seat to look at me. I did try to be brave, but I couldn't help the tears rolling down my face. I remember Pa leaning into the back of the car and wiping a tear off my cheek with a firm but kind thumb and saying gently, 'And we don't want that.' Once I was safely inside the school with chin held high, he would head for home, shedding – as I learned later – his own tears on the way.

The sadness of one boarding-school bound departure was lightened courtesy of our dog, Baggy. Baggy had a perpetual problem with keeping her rear end clean – whether it was because her short, curly coat acted like a magnet for any bits of old twig, poo, earth or leaves, or whether it was just a matter of personal doggy hygiene, I don't know. As Pa had a lot of work to get done, my mother had elected to drive me down to Brighton. My trunk was in the boot and I was dressed in my uniform complete with hat, gloves and a lump in my throat all ready to go. We climbed into the car, and just as we were about to pull away, Pa decided to pick Baggy up and make her wave a paw. He lifted her up, putting one hand around her middle and the other under her bottom – realising too late that Baggy's rear end was undesirable in the extreme. Disinclined to get involved with any doggy cleanup operation, my mother accelerated sharply away and we watched my father's face wearing an expression of disgust recede in the rear-view mirror.

My father and I were both inveterate weepers, and would become moist-eyed over beautiful music, tragic or heroic theatre or film. Of course, any real tragedy was met in public with a stiff upper lip. One evening, we were watching a film about St Francis of Assisi while my mother was in the kitchen. On his deathbed, Francis had whispered to his devoted Brother Juniper that he was not worthy to lay on a bed and asked to be moved on to the floor. Weeping, the monk and his companions complied with this, whereupon he expired. Pa and I were holding up with some difficulty at this point, and even when the monks carried the body of Francis along the crest of a hill in silhouette against a sunset, with animals of every kind following along behind, we still managed to hold it together. But when the music swelled as a flock of birds flew across the sunset over the funeral procession, it was too much. There we sat, side by side on the sofa, howling unashamedly. At that point my mother stuck her head round the door, took one look at us, said, 'Oh for goodness' sake!' and took herself back to the sanity of the kitchen.

On the other side of the coin, Pa and I would howl with laughter over things that were slapstick, lavatorial or just plain silly. *It's a Knockout* was one of our favourite television programmes; I remember how we rolled on the floor holding our aching sides with tears of laughter pouring down our cheeks as we watched the competitors dressed as over-sized mice with strong elastic tails sliding helplessly backwards on their tummies down a greased slope while, with the tip of their tails anchored to the bottom of the slope, they repeatedly tried but failed to run up it in order to place a gigantic piece of cheese into a net at the top.

Laughter seemed to accompany my father and I pretty much everywhere we went. He was a great walker, and on most days would go for a three-mile hike over the heath near the cottage. I would often go with him when I was at home from school for the holidays, and we would set the world to rights or tell each other terrible jokes as we went. On one such day, when the jokes had been many and dreadful, and I was in danger of having the type of accident that can be brought on by laughing too much, we were on the last lap of our walk down a riding track which led into our lane. The pathway ran between two high banks, dimly lit due to the small amount of light penetrating through the leaves of the trees which grew on either side. You could walk either in the narrow, sand-filled gulley – which was difficult and meant your shoes would fill with sand – or you could straddle the sandy stretch and walk with your legs wide apart and your feet placed on either side of it – a spread of about four feet but, nevertheless, the easier option. 'This track,' said my father over his shoulder to me as I followed him inelegantly along, straddling the gulley, 'was designed for very old gentlemen with diarrhoea …' Whether there was going to be more of his theory, I never found out, as I was laughing too hard to hear any more – and jolly nearly proved that my father's premise about the track applied to young girls too.

At my school in the early years, my father and mother were only allowed to visit me twice, once before and once after half term. My parents would drive down to Brighton and we would spend the morning on the now-ruined West Pier, followed by lunch at the Old Ship Hotel, then off to the cinema for a film, followed by tea – either posh tea with sandwiches and cake at the Old Ship, or beans on toast at the café with a jukebox at the bottom of Montpelier Road. The days were great, full of fun and laughter, but swallowing the beans on toast at the end of the day was always difficult with the lump in my throat that grew as the time to let my parents go drew closer. And it always seemed that just as my father was looking at his watch and saying, 'Well, we ought to be getting you back ...' the jukebox would click and whirr, and Frank Sinatra's 'Strangers in the Night' would begin to play. Like my father's old-fashioned telephone ring, I can't hear that song today without feeling a pang.

Once back at school, my ritual for dealing with homesickness was to lock myself in the loo for a good cry, and then to run a warm bath and read a few pages of a book I had brought with me from home while having a soak, whereupon I would be fine. But a problem rapidly arose during my first term when my schoolmates asked what my father did. 'He's an artist called Tony Hart,' I told them.

'What, that man on the telly?'

'That's right.'

'He's not!'

'He is!'

'Never, can't be! You're making it up!'

So I sent a letter home begging my father to come and collect me that first half term so that they could see I was speaking the truth. He did, they saw, and I was; and for the most part, it did me no harm at all. There was one teacher, though, who took my class for art for just one day in that first year, and seemed to take a great delight in holding up my picture for everyone to see and going to great lengths to tell everybody how bad it was. It was no masterpiece certainly, but it wasn't that dreadful. I can only assume now there was some sort of jealousy going on, but it was unkind behaviour that at the time I couldn't understand. She was, however, the exception, as the rest of the teachers were wonderful.

My grade C result for my art O level eight years later, however, was a disappointment not only to myself and my father, but also to my art teacher, Miss Freeman. I had chosen a title of 'Sleep', and produced a picture in pen and ink with watercolour wash of a small boy asleep among the roots of a gnarled tree, with fields and hills behind, and two sides of the picture framed by the tree and its branches. I knew it was good because some of the younger pupils, creeping past the art studio where the exam was taking place, grinned and held up discreet thumbs as I glanced round at them. On receipt of my grade, I wrote to Miss Freeman who replied that it was a rotten result and the reason was most likely that the medium I had chosen was a bit too avant-garde – apparently the examining board liked powder paint. Pa and I wrote them off as philistines.

My artistic inspiration is, of course, my dad, and I would emulate his line drawings and cartoons – always choosing a felt-tip pen in preference to brushes and paint. My father's inspiration, however, was infinitely broader. Aside from everything around him – plants, trees, rocks, fences and brickwork – he loved the Italian Renaissance artists, citing Leonardo da Vinci's *The Virgin and Child with St Anne* as his favourite painting. He also very much liked Toulouse-Lautrec, his *La Modiste* painting in particular – although it was a print of Lautrec's *Aristide Bruant* that hung on his stairs. And he adored Ronald Searle – his *St Trinian's* schoolgirl characters, of course – but especially Searle's *The Raft of the Medusa* drawing, which is a gloriously wicked interpretation of Théodore Géricault's oil-on-canvas painting of the same name. While my father liked these pictures from an artistic point of view, he also found them interesting because of what had gone on behind their creation. For example, he loved *The Virgin and Child* principally because of the expression on the faces of the two women who are featured in it, but he also found it remarkable because it was Leonardo's first painting after a long period of about eight years during which, although he had been busily involved in bronze casting, architecture and engineering, he had not picked up a brush.

Paintings and drawings aside, my father also admired Henry Moore's *Reclining Figure* sculptures and was especially fond of the geometric designs of Islam. I asked him once if he had ever seen a picture that made him cry. He told me he had, and I wish I could remember what the painting was and who it was by, but I can't. It was a piece of work, probably religious, that had had to be painted in secret and kept hidden. Over a long period of time, the painting travelled great distances and was lost and found many times. Eventually it resurfaced and was put on display in a museum in a small French town. My father knew the story of the painting, and when he saw it, and saw that it was not large and flamboyant as he had anticipated, but small and dark and unassuming, it made him cry.

While I found them odd and a little disturbing, he also liked certain artworks created by a group of mentally handicapped children – a figure sporting several legs (which hung in his studio until his death), a printed red lobster and a strange multi-coloured butterfly. Another picture by a young artist he particularly liked was of a small schoolboy walking through an autumn wood, kicking leaves as he went. The artist was me – aged about 15.

It could be said that my father was prone to exaggeration. I was home from school for the summer holidays one year, playing with newts in the fishpond that my father had built, and Pa was mowing the lawn with a rotary mower, wearing his Wellington boots. Suddenly, he stopped pushing the mower and shouted my name. I trotted across to find him leaning on the handles of the mower, ashen-faced. 'Go inside, and tell your mother I've cut my toe off,' he said. I went into the kitchen and diffidently repeated this message to my mother. We both went outside and found his position unchanged. 'Can you push the mower off your foot?' asked my mother. Staring grimly straight ahead, Pa pushed the mower slowly away from him. 'I can't look,' he said, 'you'd better call an ambulance.' My mother surveyed the wound. 'It is serious,' she said. 'You've chopped the top off your Wellington.'

The garden itself featured many times in my father's programmes. One day the unit came down to film an abstract landscape for *Vision On* made from slabs of paving stone, rocks and sand, which were to be laid out on the forecourt in front of the garage. The design was big and the plan was to set up the camera on the flat roof of the garage and film Tony putting all the pieces of stone into position to make the picture. There were two problems with this. The first was that my father had hurt his back and couldn't lift the larger paving slabs, and the second was that there were so many pieces of stone involved in making up this complicated design that he couldn't guarantee putting the pieces down in the right place first go. Clive Doig, the director, had a think and then came up with a brilliant solution. He told my father to put the complicated sections of the design together taking his time, and then, using me to help him carry the bigger pieces, filmed us walking backwards as we took the stones away one by one. By running that piece of film backwards – hey presto, there we were putting the design together, positioning each stone perfectly. If you were to look very carefully at the film, however, you would see in certain sections that my father and I were walking a little oddly, as we were putting our feet down toes first as you do when walking backwards. The landscape was finished off by placing an abstract sun in the sky made from a circle of sand surrounded by small rocks and finished with a finger-drawn swirl.

Whenever there was filming being done at the cottage, rather than breaking for lunch and driving to one of the local pubs, my mother would always provide lunch for the crew – generally plump grilled chicken wings with a mustard sauce, potatoes and salad. The dining table would glow with polished glasses and Pa would pour wine unstintingly. Chris Tandy, my father's producer for the later episodes of *Hart Beat*, *The Art Box Bunch* and *Smart Hart*, recalls that it was a good plan to get as much recorded in the morning as possible, as there was never quite the same amount of energy available to get started again after one of these convivial lunches.

Ever since I was a little girl attending any of these lunch parties, I had always been given a small glass of wine mixed with water. The thinking behind this on behalf of both my parents was that if I was used to drinking a little alcohol from a young age, I would be unlikely to overdo it when I was older. (I'd like to say that this was the case, but that would not be entirely true.)

But there was one occasion when my father fed me rather a lot of undiluted alcohol – strictly for medicinal purposes. I was 12, and the family was due to travel to Folkestone to attend the wedding of one of my mother's cousins, leaving directly after lunch. I had elected to spend the morning with my friend Susie who was a keen horse rider and whose family owned two ponies. Suffice to say we went riding that morning and, making our way back to the paddock, I foolishly encouraged my mount to gallop – something I had never done before. Hurtling across a field I suddenly became aware that my pony was heading straight towards a tree. Sawing on the reins and yelling 'Stop!' served no purpose, and when my sensible mount swerved at the last minute, my feet flew out of the stirrups and I hurtled hip-first into the trunk of the tree. Crashing to the ground, I lay there writhing and moaning while my trusty steed came to a halt and trotted back to my side to peacefully pull at the grass by my head. Susie took control, picking me up and dusting me off, putting the ponies away and then helping me to limp home. Staggering into the cottage, I was exhorted to hurry up and eat lunch, as we had to be on our way. What actual injury I had sustained, I never found out, but the pain I endured during the journey to Folkestone was excruciating. The following day, the day of the wedding, was no better and trying to walk without moving my right hip was ungainly to say the least. My father looked at me with concern. 'Sometimes,' he said, 'rather than fighting the pain it is better to let it hurt.' So I tried to walk as normally as I could, letting it hurt, and somehow got through the church ceremony. Then it was on to the reception where Pa promptly parked me behind a large potted plant and slipped me three glasses of champagne in quick succession. That, I have to say, was infinitely better than the advice to 'let it hurt', and within a very short period of time, I felt no pain at all!

As well as providing a useful location for filming, the garden was also a haven for an enormous range of wildlife, including deer who, to my mother's fury, ate the roses, moles who, to Pa's fury, dug up the lawn, and frogs. My father had a thing about frogs – he didn't like them when they grew too big, although he was perfectly happy handling tadpoles and tiny frogs. I remember we were watching television one summer's evening after supper and Pa, deciding to go back to his studio to work for a bit longer, went out by way of the front door rather than going through the kitchen. No sooner had he opened the door than he came tearing back into the sitting room with a look of horror on his face. 'Jean!' he yelled to my mother, 'Come quickly! There are thousands of frogs on the lawn outside!' From her seat on the settee my mother raised a quizzical eyebrow. 'Thousands?' she asked. 'Well, hundreds!' exclaimed Pa. My mother got up off the settee and went to the front door. Seconds later she came back into the sitting room. 'How many were there?' I asked. 'Two,' she replied succinctly. With an injured expression Pa took himself off to his studio with our laughter ringing in his ears. Some time later I found the perfect gift for him. It was a mug with a small green ceramic frog stuck in the bottom of it. Naturally I didn't wrap it up to give it to him, I made him a cup of coffee in it and hung around while he drank it. His roar of disgust as he discovered what seemed to be a frog in his mug was hugely satisfying.

At the house in Esher, my father's studio had been in what would have been the spare bedroom, but as there were only two-and-a-half bedrooms at the cottage (the tiny half-bedroom which we called 'the Cell' became mine at Christmas when the grandparents came to stay), it was obvious that another room was needed for Pa to work in. Attached to the kitchen was a glasshouse – far too plain and dilapidated to be called a conservatory – but with excellent light and not too many draughts. Here Tony set up his drawing board, while paints, pencils, inks and paper were stored on crooked shelves and in old sideboards. The existing kitchen was very small but had an extraordinarily high ceiling rising to a point which my father and I, roaring with laughter, would use for trying to set a record for fishcake tossing.

Eventually, my mother declared that the kitchen was far too small, and it was decided that the glasshouse should be knocked down to allow the kitchen to be extended and a large shed be erected in the garden to serve as a studio. It was a splendid shed, which was warm and dry and much bigger than the glasshouse, with only one old sideboard for storage and plenty of new purpose-built shelves. While the shed had electricity for light and heat, it did not have any running water, so Pa would beat a path to the house for water supplies and the loo. My mother and I would, of course, beat our own paths to the studio in order to provide him with tea – into which he would invariably stir his paintbrushes while sipping at his paint water. But at last the day came when my parents agreed that the finances would stand the building of a brick-built studio, with lots of windows and skylights, and huge flat drawers in which to keep paper and finished artwork – and running water. Any visitor to the house always loved to see the studio – and indeed Pa always loved to show them – which was usually kept in a state of organised chaos with the current project spread all over the large central table. Cupboards down one side held paints and inks, and a vast plan-chest held paper and card of untold variety and colour. There was a phone and a fax, and a sound system in the corner that played records, cassettes, CDs and radio. When my father was working on something that was minutely detailed and required great concentration, he would have background music playing – light classical stuff in general, and Lesley Garrett in particular. On the other hand, he would focus on radio plays, opera or tapes of *The Goon Show* while he was occupied with the artistic donkey work of laying down washes, colouring or filling in.

My father had many passions – food, my mother, books, me, music – and not necessarily in that order. I must have been about five years old when I remember Pa being very excited about a new thing called the Bossa Nova, and the jazzy samba rhythms played by the Dave Brubeck Quartet would float through our house in Esher. Pa was no musician himself but greatly appreciated the talent in others. He shared my mother's enthusiasm for musicals – two of his personal favourite numbers being 'A Fool Sat Beneath an Olive Tree' from *Kismet* and 'Crazy World' from *Victor Victoria*. He loved Bernstein and Gershwin, and he adored Canteloube's collection of *Songs from the Auvergne*. I don't believe there was any classical composer he did not like, but Tchaikovsky had to be at the top of his list. He showed me how a conductor would wield his baton for the different time signatures – down, right, up movements for three/four time, and down, left, right, up for four/four time. He and I would stand in the kitchen, each brandishing a chopstick in proper fashion, bringing in the sections of our invisible orchestras with verve and passion – and occasionally at the right time. Our 'Marche Slave' had to be seen to be believed!

My father was pretty well organised in his work – always keeping a comprehensive diary of engagements and deadlines, and always ensuring he had sufficient materials before embarking on a new project. He rarely forgot anything – but if he did, it was spectacular.

Next to the garage was a small dark outbuilding that became my father's film shed. With an 8mm film camera mounted on a wall bracket above a rostrum, Tony would create his own stop-frame animated films; it was fiddly and time-consuming work. A drawing with cut-out pieces that could be moved independently would be laid beneath the camera, then the button to run the camera would be pressed and held for three seconds. Then the section of the drawing that was to appear to move would be shifted a millimetre or two and filmed for another three seconds, and so on. My father spent three days in the shed filming a complicated piece of animation, and finally came out exhausted but happy with what he'd done. The following morning, he went to remove the film from the camera to take it to be processed, only to discover that he had made a fatal error – there was no film in the camera.

In 1977, a short while after my father's new programme *Take Hart* had started, producer Christopher Pilkington decided another personality was needed for Pa to relate to. Because of his knowledge and understanding of stop-frame animation, when Christopher introduced him to David Sproxton and Peter Lord and their concept of a little animated Plasticine character called Morph who lived in a wooden pencil box and who was going to co-star alongside him, Pa embraced the new idea unreservedly. Christopher and my father would have their meetings in the studio at the cottage – so much better than at the offices at Television Centre, since everything Pa needed to demonstrate his ideas were to hand – and decide on the theme for each programme. The schedule for the day would be work in the morning, then lunch – convivial and gently boozy – followed by more work in the afternoon, and then tea which would gently segue into a drink or two, after which Christopher would happily but carefully drive himself home through the leafy Surrey lanes.

Shortly after these meetings with my father, Christopher would travel down to Bristol to discuss the themes with Peter and David and decide what Morph's input should be. As a rule, Christopher would ask the animators for one interactive moment with Pa and Morph together, and one action moment with Morph on his own. David and Peter, just out of university, would meet Christopher at The Rose of Denmark in Dowry Place, where over sausage and chips they would discuss and act out the ideas for Morph with Christopher taking the role of my father, Peter being Morph and David working out how they were going to achieve their objectives on film. Christopher recalls that people drinking in the pub would cast odd glances in their direction since a great deal of standing up and walking about would be going on. Once decided, life would be breathed into the little Plasticine character courtesy of a Bolex camera propped up on David and Peter's kitchen table.

The enthusiasm of these two young animators was boundless – equal only to Pa's own – and they would delight in meeting any challenge and finding a way to achieve some new effect. One storyline required Morph to walk from one side of his box to the other. Christopher wondered out loud whether Morph could jump over it. Immediately, David and Peter became consumed with working out how that could be achieved – never having made Morph jump before. Wires and string would need to be employed, and – bearing in mind that a day's work would produce only seconds of Morph animation – it would take weeks. 'Just let him walk around the box,' implored Christopher, but no, this was new ground to be broken, and both David and Peter were determined to accomplish it. And of course they did. It was Christopher Pilkington's opinion that the unbridled enthusiasm and skill of these two brilliant young animators, together with my father's own passion and talent, were the two creative sources that were the very heart of the success of *Take Hart*.

Whether they were entertaining colleagues from the television production teams, friends or family, my parents were natural hosts, and both excellent cooks, and long and many were the lunch or dinner parties that they gave for their guests. I loved nothing better than to stand alongside my father in the kitchen, chopping vegetables and stirring pots as directed, all the while discussing life, the world and everything while we prepared his legendary curry. A skill brought home from India, Pa would generally make two meat curries, one lamb and one chicken, a vegetable curry using potatoes, carrots, onions and red and green peppers, and a dhal from lentils, and there would always be a small cast-iron saucepan full of hot sauce for those who wanted to spice up their curry a bit more. My mother was queen of the poppadoms, rapidly frying them in oil and placing them in tottering golden stacks on the table. Little dishes of chutney and hot pickle, coconut and cool raita would be scattered across the table like rafts across a lagoon.

At one time, my father acquired a stainless steel dish with several small compartments that revolved – like a Lazy Susan – and was perfect for all the curry accompaniments. My son Alistair was about three at the time, and while the rest of the family were busy with a heated discussion on the influence the Beatles had had on society in the sixties, we didn't notice him dipping a spoon into one of the compartments. Our conversation was suddenly interrupted by a howl of agony and we all turned to see Alistair with tears pouring down his cheeks. For a moment we could not think what was wrong with him – until we realised he had swallowed a spoonful of fiery chilli pickle. So amid much laughter we dried and patted the little boy, and fed him several spoonfuls of cooling yoghurt until peace was restored once again.

The traditional Christmas lunch was always a delight at my parents' house – tender roast turkey with chestnut stuffing at one end and pork stuffing at the other, perfect roast potatoes, sprouts, chipolatas, bread sauce and gravy, followed, naturally, by a flaming Christmas pudding. One Christmas morning, however, when my mother was halfway through pushing chestnut stuffing up the bottom of an enormous turkey, she announced, 'I think this bird is off.' Pa went across to the kitchen table to give it a sniff. 'No, not really, I'm sure it'll be alright when its cooked,' he said. So the somewhat whiffy bird was parcelled up in foil and popped into the oven. Several hours later, it was taken out and placed on a vast wooden board. My parents regarded it uneasily as the sound of crackers being pulled by assorted hungry family members floated through from the dining room. 'It still doesn't smell right,' said my mother. 'Parts of it will be fine, I'm sure,' said Pa optimistically. So while my mother dispatched bowls of potatoes and sprouts to the dining table, my father was carving pieces of turkey and sniffing each one before sending it into one of three dishes saying, 'OK, OK, that'll do for curry, God no! OK, curry, OK,' depending on whether it smelt all right, dreadful or only slightly iffy.

Among their many friends and frequent visitors were the Alexanders: Terry the late actor – who had met my mother when they were both working on *Gary Halliday*, a drama series produced in the early days of television – his wife and their two sons, Nicholas and Marcus. Nick was a little older than I was, and Marcus a little younger. They had often visited us at the house in Esher, but they loved the cottage. Terry, genial with good food and wine, would raise his glass to my father. 'Here's to "Total",' he would say. 'Total bliss!' The boys and I, finding grown-up conversation tedious in the extreme, would stay with the adults for a polite five minutes, then Nick would say to me, 'Shall we go upstairs?' Being nine years old, I could never understand the roar of laughter from the grown-ups that followed us as we went off to play in my room.

As a dad, my father got it right pretty much every time. When I was ill and had to stay in bed, he made me milk jellies; when I had a nightmare, he brought me downstairs and fed me with Heinz Cream of Tomato soup; at bedtime, he would read to me from *Winnie the Pooh* and then tuck me in so tightly that I was trapped flat and couldn't move a muscle, and he would always leave the landing light on so that I could see the crack of light under the door. But there was one occasion when he got it wrong. I was about 11 and we had guests staying with us at the cottage. My room had been given up to an old friend of my parents who was in the early stages of a new relationship with his lady. Thinking that it would be inappropriate for me to sleep in the Cell immediately next to their room, and eschewing the sofa in the sitting room downstairs, my father decided to make a bed for me in the film shed beside the garage. The cobwebs were swept out of the corners, a bedside light was set up, and a camp bed made cosy with warm blankets and a pillow was put under the one small window, which looked out on to our neighbour's field. After supper, I bade everyone goodnight, and trailed out to my shed. It was dark, and the moonlight threw strange shadows across the path. Owls hooted and a fox barked. Nervously, I lifted the latch and let myself into my impromptu bedroom. I climbed into bed, turned out the light and, closing my ears to the noises outside that seemed much too close, almost immediately fell asleep. What seemed like only minutes later, I woke suddenly and sat up in the darkness, wondering where I was. The moon was down and I could see nothing, and then the hair stood up on the back of my neck as I heard the sound of an old man breathing raggedly right outside the small window. With a wail of terror, I leapt out of bed and fled out of the shed, across the garden and into the house where I burrowed under a pile of cushions on the sofa in the sitting room and eventually fell asleep.

My mother was first down in the morning and as she made

breakfast, I pattered out to the kitchen to join her and tell her the tale of my terrifying night. We went out to look in the field behind the shed and found the source of the midnight breathing – it was one of our neighbour's horses. As we went back into the kitchen, my father came in. 'Well!' he cried, beaming happily, 'how was your night?' Before I could reply, my mother said, 'The poor child was absolutely terrified, I told you it wasn't a good idea.' My father looked crestfallen. 'Oh,' he said sadly, 'I thought she'd like it!'

I was a reasonably well-behaved child, and caused my parents little worry while I was growing up. Determined to follow in their footsteps and make a career for myself in television, I left school at the age of 16, and went to a residential secretarial college for young ladies in Dorset for a year – not a million miles from Pa's old school, Clayesmore – the intention being to join the BBC as a secretary, and work my way up. Unleashed from the strictures of boarding school, I overreacted to my new-found freedom and frequently found myself on the carpet before the college principal, Miss Lang. To her despair, my behaviour was wild but my shorthand and typing skills were exceptional. My parents were unaware of any problem, until one evening Miss Lang telephoned them to ask if they were aware that I was going out with a plumber. There is, I hasten to add, absolutely nothing untoward about going out with a plumber – indeed it is to be recommended – but in the early seventies the college did rather pride itself on engendering relationships between the students and the local gentry or the officers from the nearby naval base at Weymouth.

The truth of the matter was that I was actually going out with a totally unconventional art student who sported dyed red spiky hair, jewellery and a wild style of dress. In order to acquire a late pass on a Saturday night, the person we were intending to spend the evening with had to come and be presented to the principal for vetting. No way would my art student pass muster – or indeed allow himself to be paraded thus before the Establishment, so I persuaded the plumber, who had a bit of a crush on me, to come for inspection by Miss Lang. He put on a tie and a suit to make a good impression and great was his distress on discovering that he had been put through this humiliating procedure only to find that the hard-won late pass was not for him. A guarded letter arrived from my father reminding me that I was only 16, and perhaps a little young to be forming any serious relationships. I wrote back immediately to reassure him that there was nothing serious about the plumber. I forbore to mention the art student, the garage mechanic, the solicitor's clerk or the naval second lieutenant.

Aside from worrying about me going wild in Dorset, my parents had a worry of their own, which they did not tell me about until after the event. Just before they were due to go off on holiday to Italy during a brief lull between series of *Vision On* in 1974, my mother discovered a lump in her breast. She took herself off to her doctor who, not liking the look of it, said she should go into hospital immediately for a biopsy and possible further surgery. With her usual pragmatism, my mother said that she would go into hospital in three weeks' time – after they came back from Italy because, as she said, if the lump proved benign then they would have cancelled their holiday for nothing, and if not – then it was unlikely that she would be going back to Italy for some time, and she would rather go and enjoy it with her body intact. My father said to me afterwards that he wondered how she was able to enjoy the holiday with that hanging over her – but she did. As he often said, she was a brave girl, my mother. On their return, it turned out that the lump was not benign, but my mother's surgeon was confident that while not having actually removed her entire breast, he had taken away enough of it to prevent any cancerous cells spreading. The first I knew of any of this was when I telephoned home one Sunday from the call box in the Royal Oak pub in Bridport. On asking Pa how they both were, he replied, 'We're alright … now!' and proceeded to tell me what had been going on. Years and years later, my father showed me a handful of beautifully posed and lit nude photographs he had taken of my mother just days before she went for her surgery. Preserving her un-marred image, I imagine.

Having been trained at college to type properly, I used to watch with amusement as Pa would laboriously type his letters on the typewriter at home using only his two index fingers. 'Two Finger Wonderboy!' I would call him and offer to type it for him. But Two Finger Wonderboy would shake his head, raise the index and middle fingers of one hand at me with a grin and carry on typing in his own sweet way. And him a children's presenter!

Around this time, along with his work for the BBC, Tony was also busy producing drawings and captions for Video Arts, a company founded by Anthony Jay and John Cleese which, to this day, produces corporate training films which are memorable for not only being informative, but particularly for drawing on humour to clarify business concepts. Many corporate types might remember the BAFTA-nominated Video Arts film *Who Sold You This Then?* in which Hugh Laurie as the character Charlie Jenkins demonstrates how not to provide engineering support to his company's clients. The original thinking behind this approach to training was that a bored audience will not learn anything – but by presenting the message in a memorable and entertaining way, they will remember the points being put across.

Indeed, my father's own maxim was that while he did not set out to educate those who watched his TV programmes, he would strive to stimulate, inform, entertain, sometimes surprise, and hopefully always satisfy. An entirely animated film made by my father for Video Arts was *The Average Chaps*, which featured a monk who, as the manager of a monastery vineyard, uses statistical trickery to adjust his production figures – using the mode, median and the mean averages to further his own arguments.

The two Tonys enjoyed working together, Tony Jay – now Sir Anthony – told me he was always impressed by the way in which my father would very quickly grasp the concept being put to him and turn it into a drawing. The relationship with Tony Jay led my father to another project – the illustration of a book entitled *The St Merino Solution*. This book was a manager's guide to profitable computing – it being early days in the age of the computer with only a few able to understand its arcane machinations – and the fictitious St Merino being the patron saint of those having the wool pulled over their eyes. My father's drawing illustrated that St Merino himself suffered somewhat from this metaphor.

In September 1974, at the age of 17, I joined the BBC and my first job was as a production secretary on the *Parkinson* programme, a chat show hosted by Michael Parkinson and based at Television Centre in west London. As my father's production office was located in the same building, we would meet for lunch at Oddi's, a little Italian restaurant just off Shepherd's Bush Green. There we would eat steak tartare and drink Chianti, and it was astonishing how many people would have contacted my mother before my father got home to tell her that her husband was having lunch with a young dolly-bird! 'Yes,' she would say, 'I know, she's our daughter.'

Television Centre was an extraordinary circular building with wings coming off it, which, as my mother put it, rather resembled a spider. My father's production office along with the rest of the Children's Programmes' department, was based in one of the wings – the East Tower – while I was up on the seventh floor of the main circular building in Light Entertainment. At the age of 17, it was a fabulous place to work, with the *Top of the Pops* office opposite and *Basil Brush*, *The Two Ronnies* and *Jim'll Fix It* just down the corridor. Many of the producers and directors that I rubbed shoulders with had been around since the early days of television, and knew both my mother and my father – so I believe that something of a paternal eye was kept on me as I embarked on my working life at the BBC.

Technologically, little had moved on since my mother had worked at Television Centre more than a decade previously. There were still no computers, no email, no faxes, no photocopiers. Everything was done by letter or by telephone, and copies of letters were made by typing on to headed paper with a carbon and a flimsy paper underneath. Scripts were typed on to a stencil, which was then taken to the duplicating department where the stencil was attached to a machine and the copies rolled off as the machine was wound by hand; they were then manually collated and clipped together.

Despite the lack of present-day technology, it is my belief that some of the best programming in the history of the BBC occurred around this time – favourites of my father's included *The Morecambe & Wise Show, The Two Ronnies, Monty Python's Flying Circus, The Good Life, Are You Being Served* and *The Fall and Rise of Reginald Perrin*. It seemed that the focus of the BBC's Light Entertainment department was to produce programmes that could be enjoyed by all the family, and shows that were funny were just that – they didn't entertain by being hurtful or embarrassing. Today, it seems that our incredible technology and speed of communication has contributed towards an unhealthy type of entertainment – I'm thinking specifically of the reality television shows that seek to belittle, shock or put down those who are watching or taking part – a far cry from my father's aim, which was to stimulate his audiences. It is, however, rather comforting that two stalwart shows that were conceived in the 1950s are still going today – *Doctor Who* and *Blue Peter*, and that the art programmes for children on our screens today are still based on the format of my father's programmes.

I spent several months working on *Parkinson* in the 1970s, and had the opportunity of meeting many of my idols – Julie Andrews, Roger Moore, Peter Sellers, Dustin Hoffman and Mohammed Ali, to name but a few – heady stuff for a 17-year-old.

One of the guests was the new up-and-coming comedian from Glasgow, Billy Connolly. On the show, he told Michael Parkinson the story of a man who had buried the body of his dead wife in his garden with her bum sticking out of the ground. Why? He needed somewhere to park his bike! The studio audience exploded into laughter, and so did my father at home when the programme was aired later that evening. So much so, the next day he drew a cartoon of Billy Connolly with his bike accordingly parked. On my next visit home a few days later, he gave it to me asking if I could get it to Billy via his agent, as he wanted him to have it. The drawing was rolled up and put into a cardboard tube, and I lovingly carried it on to the train at Guildford and tucked it into the luggage rack above my seat along with my suitcase. At Waterloo, I went down on to the underground and on to Tottenham Court Road where I changed on to the central line heading west for White City and the flat I shared. One stop along from Tottenham Court Road, however, I realised I was no longer carrying the drawing. Horrified, I jumped off at the next stop and leapt on to the next train going back the way I had come. I returned all the way to Waterloo, thinking it was all pointless and the Guildford train would have already disappeared and what was I going to say to my father, but I had to try. I raced up the stairs into Waterloo station, and tore across to the Guildford platform. At the gate I blurted out my tale of woe to the ticket collector who said, 'It's all right, the train is still here, it doesn't leave for five minutes. Where were you sitting?' Together we ran down the length of the train, stopping to look into several compartments until finally, there in the luggage rack above a lady who was peacefully reading her book, was my precious tube. Filled with relief and babbling my thanks to the ticket collector, I retraced my steps back across London, fiercely clutching the drawing all the way. The next day, it was dispatched to the agent, and shortly after that we received a call from a totally delighted Billy Connolly who had safely received the cartoon – which I am told he has to this day.

RUBBING WITH RULERS

With a pair of scissors, Tony cuts several small shapes from a piece of textured wallpaper – a helmet, a breastplate and other similar outlines to make up a suit of armour – and sticks them on to a piece of card. He adds other distinctive shapes cut from plain cardboard, which is a little thicker than the textured wallpaper – a sword and a belt on to which he has scored a decorative pattern with a scalpel. Then he places a piece of white paper over the cut-out pieces and rubs all over it with a black wax crayon; the image in relief begins to appear. Because the cardboard pieces stand proud of the textured wallpaper, they are blacker than the rest and the detail of the scoring stands out. To remove the marks where the black wax crayon has gone over the edges of the image, Tony cuts around the figure and mounts him on a rich red background. The result is a perfect brass rubbing of a majestic knight in miniature.

When somebody achieves celebrity status in the public eye, it is usually only a question of time before they are rubbing shoulders with political leaders and royalty. My father was not a great one for big parties, always preferring smaller, more intimate gatherings, and tended to avoid the celebrity bashes attended by the glitterati of the day. However, where his artistic skill could be used to raise money or awareness for those in need, he was there. And this meant he frequently found himself in the company of like-minded celebrities along with world leaders, dukes and princesses.

My father's first brush with a prime minister, however, was while he was still at school at Clayesmore. He had a friend at school called Roly whose mother worked as a secretary for Winston Churchill. It was the end of term, and Tony would usually take the train to London and then change trains to go on to Maidstone. However, Roly had asked him to stay with him in London for a day or two. They went up to Waterloo and then took a taxi to Downing Street. My father was suitably impressed when Roly spoke to the policeman outside Number Ten, who nodded and then waved the boys through a side gate into the garden and round the back of the house. They clattered up the stairs and found Roly's mother working in her office. After greeting them both, she told them to go on up to the next floor and amuse themselves until she was free.

Roly dragged my father upstairs into a room which he remembers being furnished with little more than an enormous table on which there was a magnificent train set. This kept both boys amused for some considerable time. Suddenly the door opened to reveal, instead of Roly's mother, a familiar portly figure wearing a bow tie and puffing on a cigar, regarding them from the doorway. 'Ah,' rumbled the well-known voice, 'young Roly, home for the holidays. See you're not a trouble to your mother.' As the boys scrambled to their feet in deference to the Prime Minister, he nodded to them both and walked out of the room.

Over the years, my father found himself at Number Ten Downing Street many times in connection with the various charities he supported, and rubbing shoulders with the great and the good. The charities were numerous and included Barnardos, the Cystic Fibrosis Trust, The Foundation for the Study of Infant Deaths, The Children's Trust at Tadworth, the Gurkha Welfare Trust and many more. Always a staunch conservative (he was appalled when at one general election, my mother voted Liberal), he could be a little offhand with the Labour leaders.

As a rule, he was usually to be found on his hands and knees with his bottom in the air drawing on the floor for the children, and he was thus engaged one day when he found himself looking at a pair of highly polished shoes peeking out from a pair of well-pressed trousers. He looked up and found that the shoes belonged to James Callaghan, Prime Minister from 1976 to 1979 and Labour leader until 1980. The Prime Minister seemed inclined to talk, so my father got to his feet and exchanged a few polite words with him, but then cut him short saying, 'You must excuse me, I'd better get back to the children.'

'Of course, of course,' said the Prime Minister, and hastily retreated while my father knelt back down on the floor again, to be instantly surrounded by his young audience.

He was in this exact same position when the Queen Mother came across him at Clarence House, but she was concerned that he continue entertaining the children and waved him down as he started to scramble to his feet. 'No, no,' she said smiling graciously. 'We know Mr Hart. We like Mr Hart.' The Duke of Edinburgh, however, is well known for his direct and unexpected remarks, and my father came across him several times due to his involvement with the Duke of Edinburgh Awards scheme. On one occasion, Prince Philip asked, 'Still working with Morph?'

'I'm afraid so, sir,' my father replied.

Prince Philip's eyebrows shot up. 'Afraid!' he said. 'Why are you afraid?'

'Well,' replied my father, 'they say you should never work with children or animals – I would add Plasticine to that!'

There was a long and awful silence, and then the Duke threw back his head and roared with laughter. He walked away, still chuckling and muttering, 'Plasticine, very good.'

Almost every year since its inception, my father has attended the *Woman's Own* Children of Courage Awards held at Westminster Abbey in December. Since the death of my mother, my husband and I have accompanied him, and it is a glorious, uplifting and at the same time utterly humbling experience. Ten children who have either performed acts of bravery or have borne terrible illnesses or deformities and undergone countless operations with cheerfulness and courage, have their citations read out and are photographed and presented with a medal.

Some of the children are carried up to the presentation platform, some walk and some push themselves in wheelchairs. The breathtakingly beautiful singing by the Westminster choristers, the carols that everybody joins in with, and the service itself all add to this unforgettable event. Once over, the children and guests repair to the Jerusalem Chamber, or in later years to Poets Corner in the Abbey, for a reception where they can chat and have a drink. One year, the presentations were made by Princess Diana and my father was, as ever, caught up in the Abbey doing drawings and signing autographs for children. By the time he got to the Jerusalem Chamber it was heaving with people. Hoping to be presented to the princess and pressing his way through the throng, he found himself beside Peter Bowles, an actor he knew slightly, who was talking with Princess Diana about violence on television. My father was suddenly shoved from behind and only just managed to prevent himself from crashing into the princess, who turned to look at him and, without waiting for an introduction, smiled and said, 'Well, we certainly don't get any violence on your programmes, do we?'

Another time, at the lunch in the House of Lords that followed the reception, Tony found himself sitting beside one of the Children of Courage, Josie Russell. She was a young girl who at that time had been unable to speak after her mother and sister had been brutally murdered, and she herself had been terribly injured. Who better for her to be sitting next to than someone who could draw pictures on the table napkins to make her smile, and for her to draw her own pictures in response?

I had the privilege of being with my father when he finally achieved a lifelong ambition and was presented to the Queen. For many years, Tony had been involved with the Tadworth Children's Trust – a home for very severely handicapped children which provides care, therapy, rehabilitation and special education to its young patients. The Trust was being honoured with a visit from the Queen and had invited fundraisers and other contributors to share the day with them. My father says that this must have been at the beginning of a sharp decline in his health, because his memory of the day is not the same as mine. He was frail, certainly, and could not stand for long, so while we were standing in line waiting in readiness for the Queen to arrive, I got a chair for him to sit in. Two other celebrities involved with the Trust who were also to be presented were Bernard Cribbins and Michael Aspel, and they were standing on either side of him. I was standing about six feet behind Pa, ready to whip the chair away when the Queen arrived.

Suddenly there was a commotion outside, and whispers of 'She's here, she's here!' Bernard and Michael took an elbow each and helped my father to his feet and I shot forward to grab the chair and whisk it away. In came the Queen, who spent several moments talking to the Trust's dog handlers – alongside two lovely, patient dogs each wearing a large label round their necks which bore the inscription 'Pat dog' identifying them as dogs that the handicapped children could touch, stroke and pull about as much as they liked. Then the Queen moved down the line of guests to be presented. She spoke to Michael Aspel for a moment or two and then was introduced to my father as 'the world-famous artist, Tony Hart'.

She shook hands, saying a few words, and my father gave a little bow and said, 'How do you do, your majesty.' She smiled warmly, and then moved on to meet Bernard before being whisked out of the room to go and meet some of the children. I sat Pa down in his chair again, and we chatted with Michael and Bernard for a while before being shown into another room for lunch.

When describing the event some time later, my father said that although the Queen had talked to Michael Aspel for ages – which she hadn't – she was dismissive of him, which simply wasn't the case. It's so sad that the onset of a disease of the brain can wrongly colour the memory of an event which, only one or two years previously, would have been recalled with joy and pride.

Many efforts were made by many people to put my father forward as a candidate to receive an honour for his unparalleled contribution to children's television, but sadly these never came to anything. Pa suspects that it may have been his visits to South Africa that blotted his copybook, since they were made at a time when that country was ruled by an apartheid regime. Whether this was the case, we shall probably never know, but I do know that while he certainly would have enjoyed being a CBE or an OBE or Lord Hart of Bleeding Hart's Yard, the knowledge that young people were pursuing careers in art or design as a direct result of his inspiration meant more to him than any gong possibly could.

WEST TO EAST

Tony takes up a white paper plate, stipulating that it must be the unwaxed sort. With a white wax crayon, he begins to draw a design which seems to be mainly curves and curls on to the flat centre of the paper plate – and which, being white on white, is totally invisible. 'The difficulty,' he explains as he lifts the crayon off the plate for a moment, 'is carrying on with the design where you left off.' The design complete, Tony drips a blob of blue ink on to the plate and wipes it around with a piece of cotton wool. The wax crayon repels the ink, and instantly an intricate design in white is revealed coming out of a blue background – a dragon curling its way around the plate.

Vision On was sold by BBC Enterprises, the sales arm of the BBC, all over the world, and Tony's face became well known in households on virtually every continent. It wasn't until 1976 that my father achieved a long-held ambition to visit the United States – and the trip was made not with my mother but with his agent Roc Renals, who handled all his personal appearances. This union had come about after a visit Roc paid to Japan two years previously. He was enormously impressed with some artwork produced by Japanese children and wanted to mount an exhibition of this work in England. He contacted many people to see if they would be able to help him. A producer at the BBC told him, 'You don't want me, you need Tony Hart.' Roc contacted my father and explained his project, and the two arranged to meet. They got on well with each other straight away and my father happily agreed to open the exhibition in Bracknell.

The Japanese children duly arrived in England with their artwork, and a stratagem that proved enormously popular was for them to write the closest Japanese approximation to English names in Japanese characters. The nearest they could manage for Tony Hart was 'Ton Li Har', which translates into Japanese as 'East Man Deals'. The exhibition, intended as an exercise in promoting

141

international understanding, was reciprocal, and Roc arranged for artwork from local schools to be sent to Tokyo to be exhibited there. It was the first collaboration between Roc and my father and the whole thing was a huge success. Their friendship grew, and more events followed – carnivals in Bracknell and a performance at the National Theatre. When my father confessed to the fact that he had been opening shops and making personal appearances without taking any fee, Roc was appalled and immediately took over the handling of these events, boosting my father's income significantly. When Pa's schedule became too hectic, and a request for yet another personal appearance arrived which my father did not want to do, Roc would suggest a ridiculously high fee. If those that wanted him were prepared to pay it, then of course my father would do it. Generally, however, the request would be withdrawn and Pa could have a day off with a clear conscience.

Before Roc took over the handling of these personal appearances, however, my father's commitments had been so many that they were beginning to make him ill through overwork and he sought therapeutic help. His problem was that he was unable to say no and would find himself working every weekend, opening shops and galleries, giving speeches, and drawing for charities, which, coupled with his television work, meant that months could go by without a single day off. So he found a delightful lady psychotherapist living locally who kept horses and who treated her patients at her home; he would spend a session once a week learning through roleplay how to refuse any unwanted demands that were being made of him.

'Will you judge my school's sports day?' she would ask him, and my father would smile politely and say, 'No.'

'Very good, Tony,' she would say.

'Will you help us turn the cricket pavilion into an art studio?'
'No.'

'Can you give a talk this evening to the W.I.?'

'No.'

And so it would go on, until one day my father arrived for his session to find her looking pale with an arm in plaster. Very concerned he asked her, 'What have you done?' She explained that she had broken her arm in a fall, and then to his dismay her eyes filled with tears as she told him that it was very painful and that because of it she had been unable to go down to the paddock to see her horses. Did Tony think he would be able to help her walk down to the field?

'Of course I will!' exclaimed my father leaping out of his chair. The tears vanished as she berated him, 'Wrong answer, Tony! You're supposed to say no!'

The therapy worked to a degree, but my father always felt uncomfortable about disappointing people who wanted him to do something, even though his schedule was already jam-packed. The arrival of Roc was a godsend, taking that whole aspect of his professional life off his shoulders.

So when Roc decided to take a trip to the States in 1976, he asked my father if he wanted to go with him, and was surprised and delighted when Tony said yes. So Roc contacted groups of people in America who were working with deaf children and, through his business, was able to arrange very cost-effective travel. Having also arranged three television shows and two personal appearances for my father, the two of them set off on what was to be not only my father's first visit to America, but also his first ride in a jumbo jet. In a letter to my mother, he expressed his amazement at the number of people who could be accommodated in a Jumbo and, as ever with his eye for food and drink, his disappointment with the food they were served: Chicken Kalamazoo, which he described as 'cardboard dipped in granulated cardboard.' The wine, however – a French Bordeaux – met with his complete approval.

On arrival at Chicago airport, he was astonished to find only two men at immigration trying to cope with several hundred passengers from two or three flights trying to get through at once. It took well over an hour of queuing to reach the other side – by which time Pa and Roc had missed their onward flight to Los Angeles.

Somewhat despondent, they made their way to a Polynesian-style bar tended by an unprepossessing pudding-faced blonde, showing two inches of dark roots in her hair. But she turned out to be incredibly efficient, speedily dispensing much-needed drinks with masses of ice. Eventually, they boarded the plane for the next leg of their journey to LA. Focusing on things gastronomic once more, Pa described their meal of corned beef with pancakes and spicy apple as being 'quite extraordinary', although the Bel Paese cheese and biscuits were 'all right', and he happily compared the Californian red wine to a Chilean Cabernet or Bulls Blood. Gazing down on the country west of Chicago with his artist's eye, he could see the network of roads looking like the pointing on a brick wall, every one at right angles to another forming a repeat pattern across the land. Arriving at Los Angeles, they waited in vain by the carousel for two of their cases, only to be advised finally that the missing baggage would be sent on to their hotel from Chicago. Firmly grasping those pieces of luggage that had made it through, they went in search of their hire car – a big, wallowing Ford. The car was automatic, and Pa described the traffic in LA as being like Turin, only worse, and he 'wasn't going to drive for anything'. Roc took charge, and drove them to the Sheraton Hotel, which was marvellous: 'Old-fashioned, big and comfortable. Fruit in the room, card from the management. Complete suite with ice-making machine and all. Bed seven-foot square – what a waste!' he wrote.

Deciding to sample everything LA had to offer, Tony and Roc took themselves off to a strip club on Sunset Boulevard, which turned out to be a disappointment. In his letter to my mother, my father revealed that the management had lost their drinks licence for 'gross violation of the alcoholic laws!' He added that they had probably lost their best strippers at the same time. One of the remaining girls, who had seen better days, recognised him and came over – she turned out to be from Durham.

The next day, after sampling wheatcakes with maple syrup and a sausage on the side, they set off down the freeway to Disneyland. I remember my father enthusing wildly about it at the time, and saying that his favourite ride of all was 'It's a Small World'. I went to Disneyland Paris for the first time at the age of 51, and felt obliged to visit 'It's a Small World' to see just what it was that had appealed to my father. Before the trip, I looked it up on the internet and thought, quite frankly, it seemed distinctly twee. However, when we got into our gondola and sailed off into the small world, I understood within seconds exactly why Pa had liked it so much – it is beautifully presented, utterly charming and conveys a message of peace and harmony. This is how he describes Disneyland:

> '*There's something of a religious atmosphere here – not in any way that of any evangelist, but everyone is smiling. Certainly there is a sort of paternalism coming across, but I liked it. Never have I seen so many people of all ages and all colours enjoying themselves so much – no booze, no hooligans – "if there is a heaven here on earth ..." As for the tours and the shows, it is unbelievably magic. Disney and the spirit he has engendered is probably the nearest thing to manufactured love that any of us are likely to meet.*'

Disney was certainly one of my father's great influences. He adored the films, particularly *Fantasia* and *Bambi*, and would on occasion draw some of the characters from these films for charity auctions, always being careful to sign them 'Tony Hart – after Disney'.

The next day they went on to San Diego, right on the Mexican border, staying again at the Sheraton, where my father was impressed with the high white buildings, clear water, tall palms and pelicans. He and Roc spent a pleasant evening in the lounge after dinner with a man and his three grown-up daughters who turned out to be members of the Guadalapana National Philharmonic orchestra. The following morning, after a visit to the San Diego zoo, they set off for Phoenix, Arizona.

The journey was long, and by the time they arrived at their hotel they found, to their utter dismay, that the kitchen was closed – but they were told they could have a sandwich. This turned out to be enormous slices of hot rare beef, salad with Thousand Island dressing, pickles, potato cakes, iced water and domestic wine. Roc and my father then took themselves into the bar for a drink where they found some delightful people to talk with. They drank Jack Daniels – a mistake for which my father paid in the usual way the next morning – and eventually took themselves off to bed. Nursing gently aching heads the next day, Roc and Tony journeyed on to Montezuma's Castle where they were delighted by the vast cottonwood trees and the visible strata of the red rocks. After a lunch of insipid range-style beef stew, they drove on deeper into Arizona and the Navajo country.

My father was disappointed to find the Indian children sullen and unhelpful, demanding money in return for having their photographs taken. They found an Indian arts and crafts shop; Tony was anxious to find an Indian bead headband which he wanted to include in a programme about mosaic. He found exactly what he was looking for – with a manufacturer's label saying it was made in Hong Kong. They also found some Indian blankets woven in fabulous colours and splendid patterns – made in Mexico. Somewhat disillusioned, they drove on to the Grand Canyon, which took their breath away: 'Nine miles across, one mile deep with eagles soaring below.'

They spent the night in an alpine-style hotel with a log fire in the vast entrance hall. The hotel was packed and they had a long wait for their food which, when it arrived, 'Looked fabulous as usual, and tasted of nothing as usual!' The next morning, they viewed the Canyon from various points, each one more superb than the last, as they headed towards Las Vegas. Pa described the Boulder Dam – now the Hoover Dam – as being almost vulgar, it was so big. A middle-aged American tourist standing close by said to her friend, 'Say, what is this plant?' The friend impressed my father with her knowledge of her country's monumental landmarks by replying, 'I dunno, some bridge or other.' They went into Boulder Village and into a saloon bar with, much to my father's delight, a wood walk and rails just like in the Western movies. Inside sat the Deputy Sheriff '… fat, grizzled, with rimless glasses and a gun. I was quite scared to go past him to the loo – sorry, rest room!'

They left Boulder Village and drove across the desert towards Las Vegas. Roc put his foot down on the accelerator, telling Tony to keep an eye out for police. Dutifully, my father leaned out of the window, keeping one eye on the wing mirror to watch the road behind. 'No,' said Roc, pointing a finger skywards, 'up there, bears in the air!' They arrived in Las Vegas without mishap, but my father did not warm to the place. He wrote:

'What was wonderful in Disneyland is reversed to all that is sordid, greedy and brash here in Las Vegas. I've never seen such enormous places – The Sands, Caesar's Palace, Circus Circus, The Sahara – all that Ocean's Eleven stuff! But the size, and the people, they're not real. Hundreds of thousands of slots, gaming tables, shows, all going on in a timeless state, because they never close and there is no daylight inside these monstrosities. They're not tatty – far from it – but the zombie faces and the vulgar riches displayed are quite appalling. We managed to get seats for Andy Williams's show at Caesar's Palace for $22 – then we had to bribe *the captain another $10 to get us a decent seat! Actually, the show was very good – very.'*

From Las Vegas, they made their way to San Francisco where they were to meet Betsy Ford, a woman who produced a TV programme for deaf children in the studios of the University of California. Roc had contacted Betsy suggesting that Tony should appear on her programme – and she had jumped at the idea. Having only spoken to her on the phone, Roc and my father speculated on how she would look – a bit overweight and middle-aged, they reckoned. By the time they got to their hotel Roc, having driven all the way, was exhausted and Betsy was due to turn up at any moment. 'You'll have to go and talk to her,' he said. 'I'm no good for anything but sleep.'

When the receptionist rang to say that their visitor had arrived, Tony went down alone to the lobby. He looked around and saw a very attractive young woman in her mid-twenties with long dark hair standing by the desk. She turned to look at him, and he mouthed to her across the lobby, 'You?' She nodded and smiled. That was the beginning of another long association and friendship. Roc says she idolized my father and the feeling was mutual. Pa himself says of Betsy that if there was another woman in the world other than my mother with whom he could have been happy, it was Betsy. The three of them, Tony, Roc and Betsy, spent several days together visiting schools, making the programme and seeing the sights, and when the time came to leave, Betsy drove them to the airport and kissed my father goodbye. 'That,' said my father many, many years later, 'was quite a kiss.'

Another big trip made in the seventies came about when *Your Family*, a South African magazine, contacted my father asking him to visit with a view to making a series of art programmes for one of the South African television networks. *Your Family* would pay for the trip and report on his visit for the magazine, and, once the programmes were made, send both Tony and my mother on a safari holiday to the Mala Mala Game Reserve. So they packed their bags and flew first class to Johannesburg. Finding themselves alone in the first class section of the plane, my father suggested that it was a perfect opportunity for my mother and himself to join the three-mile high club. 'Certainly not!' was her retort.

Their schedule was gruelling. They stayed at the Towers Hotel, and almost every day my father would travel to a different town where, at the local hypermarket, he would draw for, and entertain, children and adults of all colours and ages. There were radio and television interviews, and the making of the television series for South Africa – three programmes each day, nine days on the trot. On his return, I remember asking him about apartheid which, at that time, was enforced all over the country. The schoolgirl impression I had was that all the blacks were completely repressed by the whites. But my father told me that the Towers Hotel had an elderly white doorman who wore a uniform complete with gold buttons and epaulettes. One day, Pa was pleased and surprised to see a very smartly dressed black man with his family walk into the hotel, and watched the doorman tip his hat to them. 'Not the sort of thing we had been to led believe could happen,' he said.

Tony and Jean loved South Africa, and my father made many drawings of the people, the animals, the flowers and landscapes. Attending an art exhibition, he admired the work of many South African artists but was particularly impressed by the work of Keith Joubert, whose speciality was the animals and landscapes of South Africa. During one of his radio interviews, my father mentioned the work of this artist as one of the things he most admired about the country.

Each day, a driver would take my father from the hotel to the television studios where he was making his series, or to any other of his engagements, and at the end of the day would drive him back. One evening, at the end of an exhausting day, Tony came out of the studios to find a different car with three men in it waiting for him. 'We are driving you today,' he was told. 'Get in.' A little puzzled, he sat in the back next to one of the South Africans, with the other two in the front. His perturbation grew when he realised the car was not going in the direction of the hotel.

'Where are you taking me?' he asked.

'You'll see,' came the reply.

The journey went on and on, and darkness fell. Thoroughly anxious by this time, Tony wondered if he was being kidnapped, and what these people intended to do with him. After what seemed like hours, the car pulled into a driveway and stopped beside a large house. My father considered throwing open the car door and making a run for it, but he didn't know where he was or how to get back to the city. Nor did he know whether the three men were carrying guns, so he slowly got out of the car. Immediately, some lights went on in the house and a side door opened. The men gestured for my father to go with them and walked towards the door where a man was standing in silhouette with the light behind him. Tony went in and found himself standing in a kitchen. 'Follow me,' said the man. Completely baffled, my father complied, and found himself in what appeared to be a comfortable drawing room, which was full of paintings – on the walls, on easels, spread out on tables, everywhere. Tony looked around at his captors who were grinning.

'Mr Joubert is sorry he can't be here himself, but he's on his way to London,' said the man. 'He says you are to choose any one of his paintings to take home with you.' Finally realising that he was not being kidnapped, and that there was nothing to be alarmed about, my father heaved a sigh of relief, and then wandered around the room looking at the paintings. Eventually he chose a small South African landscape. The man looked at him.

'Is that really the one you want?' he asked. One of the paintings of a zebra and a secretary bird was pretty big, and was absolutely stunning.

'This is the one I really like,' began my father, 'but …'

'Then that is the one you must have,' said the man.

The canvas was rolled up, hands were shaken, and Tony was ushered back out to the car and driven back to his hotel by the three men. They told him that Keith Joubert had heard the kind words my father had said about his work on the radio, and in appreciation of this had asked his people to bring Tony to his house in order to choose one of his paintings as a gift.

'Why on earth didn't they say that right at the beginning!' said my mother when he finally got back to the hotel. She, who had been worried sick when my father hadn't returned from the television studio.

'They wanted it to be a surprise,' said Pa.

'Honestly,' she snorted, 'men can be so stupid.'

When the time came to go back to England, the canvas was rolled up, and Tony carried it as hand baggage. Unsure of its value, he decided he had better declare it at Customs. 'Anything to declare, sir?' he was asked.

'Well, there's this,' he said, and showed them the painting.

'That's very nice, sir, but not the sort of thing we're interested in.' And they waved him through.

The painting was lovingly framed, and hung in the drawing room of the cottage where it remained until my father's death, almost filling the whole of one wall.

There were other souvenirs of my parents' visit to South Africa – a circular rug made from the little hides of gazelles, another brightly coloured one featuring an abstract design of African women which hung on the wall in the book room, and several prints of African animals – all by Keith Joubert.

Both of my parents adored the safari in the Mala Mala Game Reserve that followed their weeks of hard work. My father photographed everything he saw and made drawings from many of the photos. He particularly remembers an elephant he photographed – and being delighted to see a dung beetle arrive within a minute of the great animal moving off, having left a pile of droppings behind him, the insect beginning to roll his ball of dung. Later, as they were driving through the bush, to Pa's huge excitement he caught sight of something out of the corner of his eye and called to their ranger to stop.

'I think it was a pangolin,' he told him.

'They are very rare,' replied the ranger. 'I don't think it could have been.'

But they stopped and kept a quiet watch for a while, and were rewarded when it reappeared for a split second – long enough for the ranger to verify that my father, to his delight, had indeed spotted a pangolin, or scaly anteater.

My mother, whose knowledge of politics and history was vast, was fascinated by South Africa, and while she deplored the apartheid regime, she was quick to understand the deep-rooted enmity between the different black tribes that still prevents the country from realising its potential.

Even then, the far-reaching tentacles of apartheid in South Africa stretched all the way to an editing suite in London. Although BBC Enterprises had sold *Take Hart* to South Africa, the actor's union Equity, in protest because of apartheid, did not permit British actors to work in that country at the time. Being an artist and not an actor, there was no problem about my father appearing on South African television, but Colin Bennett, who appeared as the accident-prone caretaker of Tony's studio in *Take Hart*, and was a union member, had to be edited out of all the programmes. In an interview for *The Pretoria News*, my father stated that he did not agree with Equity's attitude, and felt that the union decision was a result of minority rule. It is to his credit that by touring the towns with his workshops, Tony brought together and entertained all South African children, whatever their colour.

My mother and father visited South Africa several times, each time learning more about its people, its beauty and its excellent wine. Along with the big game, my father made drawings of the people and, with the natural observation essential to any artist, of the flowers, the birds and the beautiful South African landscapes.

In order to help a local company raise money for the South African Wildlife Association, my father mounted a travelling exhibition of children's art. Tony and Jean travelled the country, visiting many towns and cities where he would hold a workshop and then draw for the children – flying pigs or kangaroos with babies in their pouches being the most frequent requests – and auctioning off his drawings at the end of each event. Caroline Smart, a reporter for the Durban Arts Association, who described my father as an 'enchanting, exuberant and talented man', tracked him down for an interview, which was carried out at the same time as he was recording a Guest Presenter programme for Radio Port Natal. She describes his choice of music as being diverse as himself – *Greensleeves*, *Tristan and Isolde*, *Salad Days*, George Martin's theme from *Elizabeth and Essex*, and *The Mouse's Waltz* from the Beatrix Potter ballet which, she says, had him scooting around the studio on his swivel chair in a state of joyous abandon!

A second trip my father made with Roc was to Thailand in 1978 where he delighted in the friendliness of the people, and was spellbound by the fabulous architecture. A tour of many important buildings in Bangkok included the Royal Palace, and he photographed detail rather than the broader view for inclusion in his programmes. He was amazed to see a room with its walls covered in what appeared to be wallpaper with a repeat pattern, but on closer inspection discovered that the design was hand-painted directly on to the stone walls. He described the roofs of the buildings as being pagoda-like and tiled in orange and blue like a giant mosaic.

After the tour of the Royal Palace, Tony and Roc decided to walk back to their hotel, and at a wayside shrine, they bought two cages of sparrows, some flowers and joss sticks. These they offered to the Lord Buddha by laying the flowers on the shrine, lighting the incense and freeing the sparrows. They found it utterly satisfying and quite in keeping with their day. After stopping at a bar for a drink, they went in search of an eating house for dinner and, wandering through the streets, found that they were accosted by young women touting for business every few steps. In a letter to my mother, Tony writes, 'At least they sin so cheerfully here. Roc has a delightful way of saying "no" with a beaming smile – so much better than pretending you didn't hear.'

The next day, my father and Roc went off by boat on the Floating Market tour where they travelled up the most attractive but evil-smelling waterway they had ever encountered. Little islets of water plants and flowers and house boats – they saw a whole river community with floating shops selling goods in the most incredible colours – acid greens, pinks and mauves. People were washing their clothes and themselves in the river, which was fine – until my father noticed some obscene grey blown-up shapes which he suddenly realised were dead animals floating in the water. Trying to ignore the smell, they travelled up the river, stopping to photograph an elephant and a Thai girl in full traditional costume. Coming ashore, the tour guide asked if anybody wanted some soup for, there at the quayside, soup was being served to the local populace. The guide explained that it was very good soup – laced with marijuana. In his letter to my mother, my father ponders on what chef-and-food-writer Robert Carrier might have thought about that – but doesn't say whether or not he tried some. Probably not, as he was mainly preoccupied with keeping his mouth tightly shut as the longboats with powerful engines whizzed past them – showering dead animal river spray everywhere.

The next day, they toured the canals with their guide, a driver, a French family and an Australian, visiting a traditional Thai house and then a Rice Barge. The barge was beautiful and very clean with a roof and seats down either side and tables in the centre. These were laden with bananas, oranges and three fruits that Tony was unable to identify. An unlimited flow of drink was offered, soft drinks and spirits – and a cocktail called Dynamite of which the barge owners were very proud. My father described it as a mild, gentle drink that looked like orangeade. The explosion took about half an hour to arrive, in which time he had drunk three of these 'mild' cocktails – he later discovered they consisted of five parts local Thai whisky (about 40 per cent proof), one part orangeade, one part Seven Up and a dash of soda water. Tony found himself talking very solemnly to the Australian, realising with some surprise that he was rather drunk.

They went ashore to visit what appeared to be a school, where they were entertained by a display of Thai folk-dancing by the children. They had been warned that some of them would be invited to dance in what he described as a sort of Thai Conga, and that they would be chosen by the children who would wind a scarf around them. A tiny girl of about three years old caught Pa; they danced together and then bowed to each other at the end – my father thought he did jolly well in spite of the Dynamite.

The next morning, despite a hot bath and some aspirin, Tony felt dreadful, and his nose started to stream. Armed with a handkerchief in every pocket, he and Roc visited the Rose Garden where they watched Thai boxing, sword and stick fighting, cock fighting, dancing girls and elephants lugging teak in and out of the river. That evening he dragged himself to a chemist for something to dry up his nose, and a fierce little lady chemist prescribed some antihistamine for him. The next day his nose had stopped running, but he couldn't keep awake. He and Roc made their way to the airport to travel to Chiang-Mai, near to the border with Burma; he felt as if his head was full of cotton wool and could barely put one foot in front of the other.

They arrived at Chiang-Mai, and Tony noted that the country was much greener and more hilly than around Bangkok, before arriving at the hotel and collapsing into bed where he stayed for two days. The day they were due to leave Chiang-Mai, he felt much better, but now Roc was finding it difficult to lift one foot in front of the other. They flew back to Bangkok, changed aircraft and flew on to Singapore. By this time, Roc was feeling very ill indeed and barely knew what was going on around him. To my father's dismay, at Singapore's Changi Airport they had to pass through a gate marked 'Health Inspection'. Procuring a trolley for their luggage, and holding it firmly so that Roc could lean on it, they staggered through, looking like a couple of drunks.

With no accommodation booked, it was a nasty feeling to be told by every hotel they approached that it was full. Finally, the Lion City Hotel let them in – Pa described it as the usual airport hotel, second class and situated right at the end of the runway. Roc fell into bed and when my father went to visit him later on that evening, found that he had all the lights on and the radio blaring dance music. He didn't understand anything my father said to him, so Pa turned off the radio and all the lights except for the one in the bathroom, and left a jug of water within Roc's reach.

Having only just recovered himself, my father went to his own room, ordered a beer and some sardine sandwiches from room service and went to bed with a Leslie Thomas paperback. By morning, Roc was making sense again. He'd bathed and ordered tea and fruit juice, but was as weak as a kitten and in no state to go out. So my father had the day to himself. He got himself a map from the hotel reception, and headed off towards the sea. After walking for about 35 minutes, he found himself on a road beside a park that bordered the water line. There were litter bins every few yards and notices advising that a fine of $500 would be payable for littering. Tony liked it. He walked about the park looking at the trees – mainly citrus – and then went on to the sandy beach and looked longingly at the sea. He walked into the water to feel the temperature and wished he'd brought his swimming trunks. There was nothing for it but to go back to the hotel and get them. Stopping for a cola in the bar, he picked up his trunks, his book and three oranges and made the 35-minute return journey to the beach.

Tony saw there were special sections on the beach for swimming, and notices advising all the dos and don'ts – including one that said it was forbidden to change on the beach. After all that! He sat gloomily on the sand and ate his oranges, then walked over to one of the bins to dispose of the peel. A trim little policeman was standing by the bin, and bade him good morning. His English was good and my father explained his wish to swim in the sea. 'No trouble,' said the policeman cheerfully. 'You buy locker key from drinks stall.' And so it was. Clutching his key, Tony changed in a hut that had the sort of wood-and-concrete atmosphere of a seaside sports pavilion – and another policeman asleep on a bench inside it. He changed quickly, locked up his clothes and trotted out into the Pacific. Lying in the warm sea, he thought of home and wondered if all the inks had frozen in his studio.

Later that evening, back in his hotel room looking out at the city, his skin burning from walking miles in the sun, Tony finished the letter to my mother: 'The light's gone, the skyscrapers are twinkling and I don't give a hoot about my sunburn because the rest of me feels better, and I'm coming home to you on Thursday.'

Shortly after his return, my father often found that he would become tired very quickly and was falling asleep all over the place. He also found that he was frequently thirsty, and one evening after my mother watched him drink half a litre of coca cola in one go, she packed him off to the doctor. Blood tests revealed that Pa had developed late onset Type 2 diabetes – inherent in his family but probably triggered by his illness in Thailand.

INNER LIGHT

Tony selects two big sheets of thin paper, which have been painted all over with a wash of greens and blues and yellows, and places one on top of the other. Then, taking up some paper that has been painted in shades of green and turquoise and folded over once or twice to make it thicker, he cuts out long, thin shapes with scissors, and carefully positions them vertically on the big sheet. Again, using the scissors, he cuts four flattened oval shapes from thin white paper, and places two of them slightly overlapping each other, and then the other two in a mirror image.

Tony reaches for an oddly shaped but brightly painted piece of card, which he lays over the white oval shapes and we see a dragonfly amidst reeds and bulrushes. Moving away from the desk towards the light switch, he says, 'You have a look at that while I change the lighting.' The overhead lights fade while a light below the picture – which we now realise has been resting on glass – slowly comes up to reveal the dragonfly and reeds sharply outlined in silhouette while the light, reflected and glowing as if through a forest pool, filters through the dragonfly's gossamer wings.

I think it's true to say that everyone who watched my father's television programmes recognised his polite and gentle personality along with his artistic skill. But there was more to him than this. The suffering of other people – be they close friends or family suffering the torment of a personal tragedy, or those unknown to him personally living with illness or disability – affected him deeply. Where he could, he would offer words of comfort that were not just platitudes, but warm sentiments on which to build and recover after a loss. And where he could not do this, he would use his art, drawing tirelessly to create pictures for auction to raise money to help those in difficulty. His faith was a personal thing – as he said of himself, he was more religious in drawing a cartoon for the cover of the parish magazine than in attending church regularly. But faith he had – in his friends, his family and in his belief of a power greater than us mere mortals.

Take Hart started in 1977 and it was the first programme that was exclusive to Tony. Like *Vision On*, although the production office was based at Television Centre in Shepherd's Bush, the programmes were recorded at the BBC Studios in Whiteladies Road in Bristol.

Over the years, Bristol became something of a second home to my father, and during the weeks of recording his programmes he would follow the same routine. Pa would go down the day before they were due to record the show, arriving in Bristol early in the afternoon. He would take all his materials to the studio in boxes, which he had adapted to hold all the bits and pieces – one box for each design, containing three lots of everything for rehearsals, and one lot for the recording – plus additional spares just in case they were needed. The boxes were divided into compartments, with little sacks and bags that he had made to hold the materials he was going to use – these boxes were works of art in themselves. Having talked through what he was going to do with his producer, he would go and drop his suitcase off at his small but comfortable hotel and then, with a few hours to kill before dinner, take himself off to the local cinema.

The box office of the single-screen cinema in Bristol was run by two charming elderly ladies, each sporting a delicate shade of blue-rinsed hair. As the years went by, these ladies grew to know my father well, and being fully aware that he was a presenter of a children's art programme, they would personally censor for him the film that was showing. While they were happy to let him see *Fiddler on the Roof*, *Waterloo* and even *The French Connection*, when he tried to buy a ticket to see Ken Russell's *The Devils*, the ladies told him, 'Oh no Mr Hart, you wouldn't like this,' and sent him away. My father would rarely go and have dinner with the rest of the production team the evening before a day in the studio, but would take himself off to a quiet restaurant with a book to eat a solitary meal. By nature, my father was warm and outgoing and enjoyed the company of others. So much so that the reason he would not spend the evening with his production team was because he was afraid he might enjoy himself too much and have more to drink than he should, or stay up too late. He always wanted to be certain before a day in the studio that he was rested, focused and absolutely in control.

Very shortly after I left college at the age of 17, I went to spend a few days in Bristol, not only to meet up with Pa but also to spend some time with Tessa – a friend who had been at college with me and who was now working at the BBC in Whiteladies Road. While at college I had taken up smoking – a habit of which my parents were unaware, or so I thought. So when we joined my father, who in a break with his normal routine had invited one or two of his production team to join us for dinner that evening, and Tessa offered me a cigarette, somewhat to her surprise I refused. The meal progressed, and when coffee came, Tessa offered me another cigarette, and again I refused.

'Are you sure?' she asked in astonishment. Jerking my head in Pa's direction and frantically shaking it, I tried to convey to my friend that I was not smoking in front of my father. But Pa was not fooled by any of this and said, 'Look, we all know you smoke, so why don't you just enjoy a cigarette with your coffee?' So, feeling not in the slightest bit grown-up and sophisticated, but just faintly foolish, I did.

Take Hart was working well, but the producer, Christopher Pilkington, felt there was something missing. 'We need something with you,' he told Tony, 'not someone but something.' Having given this some thought, David Sproxton and Peter Lord came up with an animated Plasticine character called Morph. This character's name was a direct reference to the way he morphed himself into different shapes, but my father would refer to him as an 'amorphous lump' or 'More-fuss and bother'! Morph became hugely popular, and whenever anyone mentioned my father's name, more often than not people would say, 'Oh yes, I know him – Morph!' Morph lived in a wooden pencil box on my father's table. He did not speak, but communicated by using gestures and talking in an unintelligible squeaky gobbledegook. He was a charming little character with a feisty streak, who appeared in one-minute inserts throughout all of Pa's programmes, sometimes helping, often hindering.

In one of these inserts, Morph had made a caption for the gallery – but had spelt it with only one L. Tony looks at it and shakes his head. The animated Morph kicks the L to one side – only to reveal another one underneath. Satisfied, Tony picks up the caption and puts it in position. In another animation, Morph has apparently locked himself out of his pencil box and is seen trying to prise it open with a palette knife, but instead manages to flick himself up and over the box with a squeak of surprise. Additional characters that joined Morph in his antics were an animated nailbrush that behaved like a dog, and Chas, Morph's cousin, who was possessed of a nasty streak and was much more badly behaved. When signing autographs, Tony would always draw a cartoon animal – a dog, a cat with a fishtail hanging out of its mouth, a horse or a tiger. But by this time, everybody wanted a drawing of Morph – but Morph was not Tony's invention, so in order to meet popular demand, he had to teach himself to draw his cute but irksome Plasticine co-presenter.

My father was well known by this time, but it was a gentle fame – there certainly weren't any paparazzi hanging around the house – and it was lovely when, as often happened in a restaurant or on a shopping trip into town, one or two people would stop us to ask for his autograph. Christopher Pilkington remembers an occasion when he and my father were walking in Guildford after making a filmed insert for one of the programmes. They were walking down a narrow street when they saw a group of young men coming towards them. These men were dressed in punk style – Mohican haircuts, metal in their ears, lips, cheeks and goodness knows where else, with bicycle chains hanging off their belts – and they looked very menacing. My father said to Christopher, 'Oh dear, I'm not sure about this,' but when the punks drew closer, one stopped suddenly in their path and said, 'You're Tony Hart, you're great.'

'Yeah,' said another, 'You're cool.' And each and every one of them insisted on shaking my father's hand before they went on their way.

Christopher and Tony would have many meetings to discuss the content of each programme, and my father would work out in fine detail every artwork and design for the entire series, which would include one design for the younger children, another for the older ones and two for everyone in between.

For *Take Hart by the Sea*, Christopher suggested they film in Brighton, wanting a big beach that could be looked down upon from on high. 'Interesting,' said my father, which Christopher later told me was his way of saying no. 'How about Lynton and Lynmouth in Devon?' Christopher hadn't wanted to travel so far afield, but he went to have a look and it was, of course, perfect. The filmed piece was to start with Tony and his caretaker, Mr Bennett, having come away on holiday together, standing on a cliff top gazing out to sea across sun-warmed golden sand and telling each other what a marvellous place they had come to. The day the unit arrived to film, the rain wasn't coming down vertically – it was driving across horizontally. The sea was grey and the lowering sky was thunderous. The camera unit set up and Tony started to rehearse a picture he had planned beforehand using shells and bits of seaweed, but the wind and rain washed it away. Christopher thought it was going to be hopeless, and was ready to pack up and go home, but my father said, 'It's OK, I can do something else with wet stones.'

So they went ahead with filming the opening sequence, with Pa and Mr Bennett standing peacefully under an umbrella gazing out at a dark and angry sea telling each other that it was nice to get away for a change. Then my father climbed down onto the sand and proceeded to make a seahorse from the shining wet stones and pebbles that he found on the beach.

But the unit didn't just have the elements to contend with that day – there was also the threat of a dog answering a call of nature in the middle of an artwork. Tony had spent ages scraping a design of several giant fish onto a huge stretch of the beach, when a lone dog wandered into the area and began sniffing at the disturbed sand in that familiar fashion preliminary to a squat. The sequence, almost finished, had taken a long time to film, the crew and my father were wet and cold, and the threat of unwanted doggy decoration on the sand design for the final shot was not appealing. As the dog prepared to squat, the unit screamed in unison at it from their vantage point at the top of the cliff, while my father couldn't bear to watch. The dog sniffed, pawed briefly at the sand, and, much to everyone's relief, ran off. Recounting the tale, my father mused that the dog must have been a local art critic.

These enormous designs, or 'gigantics', filmed from high up were first of all tricky enough to accomplish in themselves, but if you consider that when the camera was positioned up on a cliff shooting down at an angle – not from directly overhead – my father had to take into account the foreshortening of the image so that it didn't distort on the television screen but appeared correctly. This was something he always seemed able to achieve instinctively – and the only time he could see if it had worked was after he had done it and climbed up to where the camera was positioned.

Many of Pa's gigantics were created by him running around on a disused airfield pushing in front of him the sort of contraption used for painting white lines on playing fields. These included one of a sheep he painted in one of the car parks at Television Centre, filmed from the roof of the building; and a 20-foot-high pin man in a fire station, filmed from the top of the tower. Other gigantics he devised were a 180-foot horse on a hillside created with soluble foam; a serpent half a mile long on a hot Pembrokeshire beach, etched with a rake and weighted with a large stone (which nearly caused Pa to black out); and 25-foot-high gaily painted flowers on the side of a riverside warehouse, which were so bright and colourful that they caused an airline pilot flying overhead to radio in to Heathrow to find out what was going on! As far as my father was aware, these gigantics were completely original – adding in an interview to a newspaper reporter, 'I don't know anyone else who would be foolish enough to make them!'

Texture was something that always appealed to my father, and he would create textures in a number of different and original ways. Sand and gravel were always excellent candidates, but mixing water-based paint with flour created a thick, sticky goo which could be used in a variety of different ways. Spread thinly over a piece of card, Pa would then scrape designs into the goo using the wrong end of a paintbrush or a cardboard comb, or dab at it with the end of a cork which would lift the sticky mixture up off the card in a wonderful prickly texture. Left overnight to dry, the flour-and-paint textured artwork would be ready to hang on the wall. Other wall-mounted pieces of artwork were made from modelling clay pressed flat and then used to take an impression of something interesting – the end of an old ship's timber, a sawn log of wood or simply the bark of an oak tree. The impressed clay would then be dried and polished with boot polish to give it a shine, whereupon it would be ready for mounting.

My father never took any of the pictures that he had made for the programme home with him. For him, it was the joy of the doing, not the completion that was important, and he would leave the finished artworks in the studio when the recording was over. But these never found their way into the rubbish – members of the crew would have pounced and spirited the artworks away long before the cleaners arrived. There was just one occasion when a piece of artwork that Pa had devised and practised countless times in his studio at home simply refused to work in the television studio. It was a collage made from corrugated cardboard and it went wrong on the first rehearsal. After two more rehearsals, it still wasn't going right and my father was becoming more tense and angry with himself after each attempt. Finally, Christopher Pilkington went down onto the studio floor to talk to Pa.

'We'll try it once more,' he said, 'and if it still doesn't work, just say "well, it seemed like a good idea at the time"!' So they set up to do the piece one more time, and yet again it went wrong. With a wry smile and a lift of the eyebrows, Pa said the words that Christopher had instructed him to say, totally understanding that for him to be seen to stumble showed that sometimes even for the great Tony Hart it was about the making, about having a go that was important – not the end result.

A piece of action art that I loved for one of his programmes proved to be a painful experience for my father. Conceived well in advance of the recording in the studio, the artwork was to be a huge firework display created on a vast piece of blue paper laid out on the studio floor. Once a city skyline had been set down in black paint, fireworks were added in streaks of yellow and red, with stars printed in white using the edge of a piece of card. Flicking coloured paint with a large paintbrush created the effect of more and more starbursts and rocket trails. Morph joined in at this point, appearing to hurl paint from both of his hands, which, naturally, hit my father square in the face with a satisfying double splat. Undaunted by this, my father rapidly bounced a tennis ball dipped in white paint across the artwork, creating random blobs of white; next he ran, pushing a roller over it and then, with a paintbrush in his mouth, was dragged on a small trolley across the paper, leaving a trail of paint as he went. Finally, by using the new stop-frame animation technique, Pa whizzed around the artwork on his bottom and then vanished, appearing to explode in a pool of coloured paint. In order to achieve this effect, my father had to sit on the artwork with his feet and hands in the air, holding the position for a few seconds while he was filmed. Then he moved along a little way, and held the position again, repeating the process so that he appeared to whiz around the entire artwork. The finished effect is hilarious, but it took ages to do, and as my poor dad was suffering with shingles at the time, holding those positions was uncomfortable in the extreme.

There weren't many occasions that my father was ill when he was recording his programmes – indeed, if I developed a cold, my mother would keep me out of his way so as not to infect him – but when he was involved in a bad car crash the day before he was due in the studio, the show still went on. It happened just outside Fleet in Hampshire when Pa was on his way to Bristol, driving fast down a straight clear dual carriageway. He had registered a car way ahead in the distance that had paused in a road off to the left, waiting to turn on to the highway ahead. Pa swept down, and then to his horror, the car suddenly pulled out right in front of him. Pa slammed on the brakes, slowing his speed a little, but he crashed full tilt into the rear of the car as it emerged, and, for a short while, knew nothing. Moments later, he came to his senses to find he had given himself a deep cut on his forehead just under the hairline, where he had hit his rear-view mirror – no seat belt laws in those days.

Very quickly, police and ambulance arrived. The driver of the other car was unhurt, but both vehicles were written off and my father was whisked away to a nearby hospital in the ambulance, with its blue lights flashing. They stitched up his head, and told him they were admitting him for the night. 'I can't,' said Pa, 'I've got to get to Bristol, I've got a programme to make!' Against their advice, my father discharged himself, and by taxi and train made his way shakily to Bristol and the little hotel that he always stayed in. Shocked and undoubtedly concussed, he put himself to bed, and the next morning went by taxi to the BBC studios.

My father's usual make-up requirement was just a darkening of his eyebrows – which were always very fair and disappeared altogether on camera – but this time, it was quite a job. The make-up artist carefully made him up, masking the area around the ugly stitched wound with foundation, powdering it and then gently arranging his hair so that it didn't show. Everyone by this time knew what had happened, and Pa was treated with great gentleness and, somewhat to his amazement, he managed cope with everything.

The following day was the end of term for me, and my mother had picked me up from school and told me worryingly that Pa had been in an accident but that he was all right. Then, having dropped me at home after an anxious journey from Brighton, she went to pick him up from the station. They arrived back about half an hour later, and at first I was shaken to see Pa looking pale with bruising around his eyes, but he was perfectly cheerful and very glad to be home. Satisfied that his injuries were not life threatening, I then watched with the delighted ghoulishness of a 13-year-old as he carefully lifted up his hair to show me his horrible wound. It healed rapidly leaving only the faintest scar, invisible under his hair. He took no extra time off, and the only long-lasting effect the accident had on him was that from that moment on, my parents always flew all the way to Italy for their holidays – their days of driving very long distances were over.

It wasn't long after this that Norman, Pa's adored father, died. He and Evelyn were looking after the cottage while my parents took a few days off among the lakes in Cumbria in the midst of a hectic work schedule. They were having dinner when Tony's brother Michael telephoned with the news. 'I'll come straight home,' said Pa. 'Don't do that, old chum,' said Mike. 'We'll start making arrangements, and you come back in a couple of days as planned.'

My father told me that he didn't weep until the following day when he took himself off for a long, solitary walk high up in the hills. Coming across a lump of rocky strata pleasing in shape and size, Pa began to scratch on it as deeply as he could with a small, sharp stone, working away at it for some time. At last, satisfied with his work, he walked back to the hotel where my mother was waiting for him and, to his surprise, he found that he was able to enjoy the remaining two days of their holiday. In later years, whenever he and my mother returned to that part of the country, he would always take a big masonry nail with him and, making a pilgrimage to the rocky outcropping, would deepen the scratches he had made. Walkers today climbing the fells of Cat Bells high above Derwentwater just might come across a rock which has a deep 'N' inscribed in it, my father's personal memorial to his own beloved father.

The years went by, and when I was 20, Will and I decided to get married. I telephoned Pa – going through our normal ritual of him singing the number and me singing 'Papa!' – and asked if I could go down for lunch and bring Will with me, so that he could, unbeknownst to them, formally ask my father for my hand in marriage as tradition demanded. In fact they knew something was in the wind, principally because I almost never brought any boyfriends home to meet my parents, and the fact I was bringing this one to lunch was a bit of a giveaway. I remember nervously slicing runner beans in the kitchen with my mother while Will, equally nervously, went out to talk to Pa in his studio. But the nerves weren't necessary. Permission was happily given, champagne was opened and we gave ourselves over with gusto to discussing the details of our forthcoming nuptials over a long, boozy lunch.

There was only one person who we wanted to perform the marriage ceremony, and that was one Captain the Reverend Cuthbert Le Mesurier Scott RN. This was a man who my father had first met at a party at George Martin's house in London. He had been introduced to this ecclesiastic who sported a beard and moustache reminiscent of Don Quixote, with twinkling eyes and a charming, bashful manner, and who was shortly to leave his parish of St John's, Hyde Park Crescent, to move to a small village deep in the Surrey hills.

'We live in Shamley Green,' my father told him.

'That's where I'm going!' exclaimed Cuthbert, and so began the start of a friendship that was to last to the end of their days. Cuthbert had spent 30 years in the Royal Navy, and then went into the Church for another 30. Years later, he told us how on first arriving at the parish of St John's, he felt compelled to visit as many of his new parishioners as possible to introduce himself to them. As he walked up the path to each house, he told us, he would pray. 'What did you pray?' we asked him. 'That they would be out!' he replied with his bashful smile.

For my father, Cuthbert was the perfect vicar. They shared the same beliefs and many opinions, and my father's admiration for this naval captain-turned-ecclesiastic knew no bounds. Kindred spirits, they shared the same enthusiasm for their chosen callings. As the years at Shamley Green rolled by, my father opened the Church fetes, led the budding artists who took part in a great, messy painting extravaganza held inside the church itself, and every month drew a cartoon for the cover of the Church magazine. Usually this was a caricature of one of the villagers – and on one occasion he drew a cartoon of Cuthbert himself chasing out the devil in the form of an ink blot. Behind the bashful manner, Cuthbert was razor-sharp and was wont to use a turn of phrase that could, being a vicar, take one by surprise. On the question of whether or not to promise to obey in my marriage ceremony to Will, Cuthbert told me, 'All the way through your marriage you will have to make decisions, and sometimes you won't agree.' As we sat in the front pew in the hallowed empty quiet of Christ

Church, he continued, 'It's always easier if someone has got the casting vote so you can say, "Alright you swab, you bastard – we'll do it your way"!'

Of Pa's cartoon of himself, he wrote the following in his vicar's letter for that very parish magazine:

'I had wished to be regarded as worthy and dignified, and the great Tony Hart (blast him – take him off and burn him) sees me as a sprightly ant, purposeless. What does an irrelevant ant do in Church? Perhaps laugh a bit, or cry? Or fall in love with someone – or listen to those astonishing words saying that our irrelevance is washed out by the love of God? But it might be risky; it might mean exposing yourself a little – letting go the hope one has of being seen as a helpful, powerful, advising sort of person. Next month it will be different. Mr Hart is dealing with another Parishioner. I wonder how he (or she) feels now!'

This does, I think, give a flavour of this man of whom my father thought so highly. Pa was not, as Cuthbert very well knew, portraying him as an irrelevant ant, but had set out to capture something of the enthusiasm and energy that this marvellous man put into everything he did.

So plans for a wedding at Christ Church, Shamley Green, with Cuthbert performing the marriage ceremony were set in motion. As a gifted musician, Will announced his intention to write all the music, with a piece for me to walk up the aisle to, another piece for himself and I to walk down the aisle to, and a special piece to be played during the signing of the register, which was to be a fugue based on *The Sailor's Hornpipe* written expressly for Cuthbert. And so it was. On the day, we completed the paperwork before the fugue was finished, and I remember standing beside Will facing Cuthbert who was jigging on the chancel steps with utter delight to his own piece of music – and into which Will had even woven the celebrated phrase from *Rule Britannia.*

There were others who wanted to be involved in our wedding – including our postman Peter Parfitt. He had been bringing letters to our house since I was a teenager, and as I grew a little older, I would lean out of my bedroom window, hopeful for a letter from an admirer – which sometimes there was, but mostly there wasn't. As I leaned out, Peter would go down on one knee beneath my window crying, 'Juliet!' I would reply, 'Romeo!' and he would hold out his hands signifying that there were no love letters for me. So we would grin at each other and he would go back down the garden path, stopping in at Pa's studio to chat and look at whatever my father was working on. On the news of my forthcoming marriage, Peter went to my father to formally ask if he could drive me to my wedding. This was readily granted, and Pa insisted that he drive our own car bedecked with ribbons. Peter's wife Peg had asked if she could remain at the house ready to welcome us when we got back from the church. My father thought this was a very good idea, and gave Peg strict instructions to have ready for Will a glass with a shot of excellent whisky as soon as we got back. 'He'll be needing that!' he told her.

Although invited as a guest, Massara, my father's old friend and the banqueting manager at the Hyde Park Hotel in Knightsbridge, had announced that he was going to organise the food for the reception. This was to be a wonderful, informal affair in the garden at the cottage, with Massara winding his way through the throng of friends and relatives bearing great trays of canapés.

But while all these preparations were going on, all was not quite well with Pa. Ever since his illness in Thailand, his hair been falling out and was much thinner than it usually was, and, although he was not an overly vain man, his snowy white hair was one of his most distinctive attributes and he was desperately upset about it.

The day before the wedding, we both went to his hairdresser to have our hair done. He had the experienced stylist and I had the trainee. We sat side by side in front of the mirrors, and he was hugely comforted by his hairdresser, who told him that she could see that new baby hair was beginning to grow, and that she would be able to blow dry his hair and style it so that it would look as thick and luxuriant as ever.

So preoccupied was I with watching what was going on with Pa, I was not paying attention to what was happening to my own hair and found, to my horror, that my trainee hair stylist had cut it much shorter than I wanted. It was, I have to say, the first and only time in my life that I have ever cried over my hair. When Pa and I got home I raced upstairs to wash it furiously in the vain hope that I could stretch it by a millimetre or two. My haircut could have wrecked the whole occasion, but it didn't look too bad, and I didn't want to spoil the last night of being with my parents as their unmarried daughter. So, with my hair firmly put to the back of my mind, we spent a happy evening eating my mother's fabulous roast duck with crusty French bread and salad, and Pa opened a bottle of my favourite red burgundy, Fleurie.

The next morning dawned bright and sunny, to our vast relief as our wedding guest list depended on it – there would not have been enough room in the cottage to hold them all if it had been wet.

The first person to arrive was Massara, who instructed me to go and pick some parsley with which to decorate his trays. Up to that point I had been feeling distinctly useless, and leapt about my task with alacrity. 'That's plenty,' he said when I came back into the house with a handful. 'No, I'll get you some more!' I said, ecstatic to have something to do. Next to arrive were my three bridesmaids driven by Tim, the best man, who had dropped Will off at the Red Lion in Shamley Green. Not wanting Will to be waiting on his own for too long – he might have had time to reconsider! – I begged

Tim to get back to him as quickly as possible. The house was a flurry of activity with bridesmaids changing into their dresses, the cake arriving and the rest of us trying to get ourselves organised. At last I was dressed and came down the stairs to find my father, looking very distinguished in his grey morning dress, standing at the bottom waiting for me. It must be the same for any father looking at his daughter in her wedding dress on her wedding day, but for a moment or two he could not speak. Then I crossed my eyes and stuck my tongue out at him, and we burst into laughter. Into the car we got, with Peter carefully handing me in, and Pa and I drove to the church holding hands very tightly. Halfway there Pa said, 'Are you quite sure? We can turn around now if you want to.' I told him I was positive sure, and moments later we arrived at the church. Pa and I slow-marched up the aisle to my very own entrance music to where Will was waiting at the top with Tim at his side, and Cuthbert, order-of-service in hand, stood twinkling with bashful merriment at us all.

With me safely married off, work for my father continued apace. He would often be asked to attend fund-raising events at schools and hospitals for which he would spend hours sitting at a table with a perpetual queue of children waiting to have their autograph books signed. They would crowd round him to watch what he was doing, and on more than one occasion one of the children would have a small problem with wind – usually silent, but not always. Pa always wanted to say to anyone arriving at his table and encountering an unmistakable odour that it wasn't him!

Rather than just signing his name, my father would also fulfil the requests of his young admirers by drawing cats, bears, pigs, elephants – whatever they wanted, and after two or three hours of this, his arm and neck would begin to stiffen and he would develop a headache. The difficulty was always how to extricate

Sketching a giraffe in Mala Mala.

Above left: Woken from sleep to pose as a model for a poster intended for an appeal on behalf of the starving children in Biafra.

Above right: As a photographic model this time, terrified of spoiling the letters!

Below: The proud father of the bride.

A handful of Pa's cartoons and logos (from *above left*, clockwise): A pen and ink drawing of Cuthbert chasing out the devil; St Merino – the patron saint of those having the wool pulled over their eyes; Abbot on the wall of the old film shed; a Chinese Mandarin… with an umbrella sticking out of his ear!; the dragon logo for Sir Paul Getty's XI; Pa's original design for the now iconic *Blue Peter* ship.

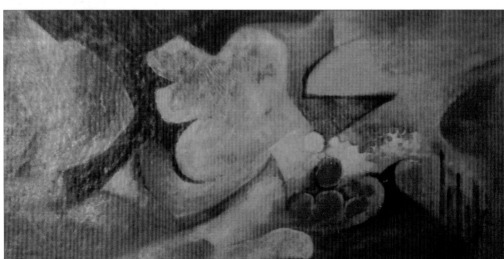

Above: Hattie and 'Toto' drawing in the studio.

Below: Pa's sympathetic abstract created for brother Michael… who was suffering from haemorrhoids!

Four of Pa's favourite pictures, by Ronald Searle (*top*),
a young handicapped artist (*above left*), Leonardo da
Vinci (*below left*) and me (*below right*).

Above: *Hart Beat* – shades of Oliver Hardy, with Gabrielle Bradshaw.

Below: With Kirsten O'Brien in *Smart Hart*.   *©BBC Archives*

Above: Into the shadows, but my old firework still sparkles.

©*Maree Aldred*

Below: Unable to eat or drink, but happy to be with old friends the Capraro family in Positano.

Above: At the funeral, everyone got involved to create this masterpiece.

Below: In memoriam, a flashmob of Morphs appeared outside the Tate Modern in London.

himself without appearing rude, because the queue of children never seemed to end. In the early years, my mother would take on the role of the bad guy, and tell the children that he had done enough and had to stop, but this always gave rise to muttering and bad feeling. Later on we hit on a plan that seemed to work. My mother, Will and I would simply join the queue, and when we got to the front of it, we would form a small barricade from behind which my father would make his escape. We then moved away, and, to the puzzlement of the children still in the queue Tony would have vanished.

Exhausted by these events, we would generally go out for dinner afterwards – in Surrey, favourites were either a Chinese restaurant in Cobham or an Indian one in Cranleigh. One evening, after successfully extricating my father from a long afternoon at a local fete, we found ourselves slumped at a table in the Indian restaurant. Trapped in a corner seat, Tony announced, 'Blast, I haven't done my insulin jab.' Will and I stood up to let him out, but he stopped us saying, 'It's OK, I can do it here, straight through my shirt,' and he discreetly proceeded to do so. Regarding my father's dexterity with the hypodermic, Will remarked, 'Well, this is nice, here's a world-famous children's TV personality shooting up in the corner of a restaurant!'

Although my father was very well known indeed by this time, he never forgot his roots. As well as revisiting his old school Claysmore and supporting Maidstone Art College, he never forgot his ties with the Gurkhas and attended many events. At a curry lunch held at the Gurkha barracks at Church Crookham, he found himself in enormous demand drawing cartoons for the many young folk who were also present. Tom Blackford, the editor of the *7th Regimental Journal,* was so impressed by this that he asked my father if he would do some cartoons to illustrate one or two of the articles appearing in his next journal – an arrangement which was to go on for almost as long as Pa's resultant 40-year honorary membership of the 7th Gurkha Rifles.

In 1985, *Take Hart* finished, and *Hart Beat* began. It was a very similar programme in format, with Mr Bennett and Morph still in attendance, and it was at this time, Tony became a grandfather. My parents were regular lunch or dinner guests at our house, and when I was ten days past my due date and bored to tears, I suggested to Will that we should have some people over for dinner. 'Who?' he asked. 'Ma and Pa?' I said diffidently. 'Of course,' he replied. So we rang them, and they were free, and instead of cleaning fridges or turning out attics, which is what pregnant women who are just about to give birth are supposed to do, I spent the day perched on a high stool in the kitchen making the most complicated and intricate dinner possible – including par-boiling carefully cut red onion rings and using them to corral small portions of peas on each plate. Most odd.

Unusually, my parents, who were not generally late birds, stayed until well past midnight and my bump received a severe buffeting as Will and my father hugged each other goodbye, standing on either side of me in our narrow hallway. We waved them off and went to bed. At about six in the morning, I woke up to monumental contractions. We were at the hospital by half past six, and just after eight in the morning, with Will at my side, Tony's first grandchild, Harriet, had arrived. Will went off to telephone my parents who were amazed at the news. 'That's impossible!' said my father, 'We only left you a few hours ago!'

Absolutely delighted with the cleverness of myself in producing Hattie, I asked my mother about my birth, and whether Pa had been with her. 'No,' she replied, and told me that although he had wanted to be there, she had said to him, 'Do you see me as elegant and dignified?' 'Yes!' said Pa. 'Well,' continued my mother, 'when this child is being born, I shall be neither, so I suggest you wait outside.'

But publication deadlines do not wait for the birth of babies, and in the event, my father was nowhere near the hospital when I made my entrance into the world – he was working frantically in his studio at home to meet a Packi and Tipu comic strip deadline.

It wasn't many months after my own birth that I became ill. Of course I have no recollection of this, but I took to projectile vomiting in a big way. When it became apparent that I wasn't keeping anything down at all, I was taken to hospital and diagnosed with pyloric stenosis – a narrowing in the gut, which prevents food from getting through the digestive system properly. The only treatment for this condition is surgery, resulting in a biggish scar on the stomach, and my father remembers pausing before signing the forms to allow the procedure to go ahead. 'She won't be able to wear a bikini,' he told the ward sister who was waiting for the paperwork. Somewhat shortly she told him that a scarred stomach was preferable to no life at all and he dutifully signed the forms. The operation went off without a hitch and yes, I have a huge scar on my stomach, which has grown with me over the years and no, I have never worn a bikini. I suppose it is a measure of the artist with his eye for beauty that my father's first concern was that his baby girl was going to be disfigured. I love him for thinking of it, but my scarred tummy really is of no consequence.

Although my mother and father were not particularly hands-on grandparents due to their own busy schedule, they adored their new granddaughter, and swiftly the question of a christening came up. By this time, Cuthbert had retired and he and his wife, Peggy, were living in Brighton. 'Could Cuthbert still christen Hattie?' I asked my father. 'I'll ask him,' he replied. So he telephoned Cuthbert, who said he would be delighted to christen Harriet in the nearby church they attended in Brighton. It was another beautiful summer's day, and the two godparents, my grandmother, my uncle and aunt, my parents and Will's mother all gathered at the cottage for lunch in the garden before putting Hattie into her christening dress and driving in convoy down to Brighton. There, my baby daughter submitted to the christening ritual with good grace while Cuthbert held her and poured the holy water over her little head, and the rest of us stood around in the quiet sanctity of the church, holding up a candle to represent the Light of God, and to welcome her into the Christian faith.

There was some discussion shortly after Hattie's arrival as to what my parents should be called. Grandma and Grandpa, my mother felt, was distinctly ageing, and Tony and Jean was just not right, but Toto and Jeannie was eminently acceptable. And Toto and Jeannie they remained for the rest of their lives.

Tony's granddaughter appears several times in his book *Small Hands, Big Ideas*. It includes a piece of artwork of hers where, at the age of one, having scribbled a few lines on a sheet of paper with a crayon held firmly in her little fist and articulating furiously from the shoulder, she then took to banging on a piece of paper with a pencil. My father said that for children at this age, it is not necessarily the making of the drawing that is interesting, but the noise that can be made with a pencil! He took several photographs of her in the garden making her picture – which included an involuntary grubby footprint – for his book and after the photographs were done, we sat down to lunch in the sunshine.

As it grew hotter, Tony wondered if Harriet would like to sit in some water. My parents didn't have a paddling pool, but there was a blow-up dinghy which would do just as well, so that was filled using the garden hose and my daughter duly plonked in. Naturally, the water being cold, she shrieked, so Pa went inside to get a bucketful of hot water to warm up the water in the dinghy. He poured in a little of the hot water, but Hattie was vociferous in her disinclination to sit in it, so we abandoned the idea and resumed our talking over coffee and brandy in the afternoon sun. After a while, we heard a gentle splosh, and looking round, saw our little baby girl had climbed into the bucket and was sitting peacefully in it. The shout of laughter that went up from the table startled the wood pigeons dozing in the nearby trees in the afternoon sunshine into sudden flight.

It was two years later, while my father was getting ready one spring morning to go and open a fete and draw for the children at a nearby school, that I had to ring and tell him that his second grandchild had died aged just three weeks. It was SIDS – Sudden Infant Death Syndrome, or cot death. I cannot remember what he said to me that morning, but he told me some time later that he had gone to the fete feeling dreadful for us, and somebody there had heard that he had recently had a new grandson called William and asked how he was. My father paused before replying, 'He's – in safe hands.' He came to see us a couple of days later, and it was special because up until then the house had seemed to be full of people all the time, but on this day there was only Pa. We were talking about the funeral arrangements, and my father asked, 'What will William be wearing?' I told him that he would be wearing a white Babygro with a blue bunny on it. My father looked confused for a moment, then said gently, 'I meant Will.' The mental image of my husband in a Babygro with a blue bunny on it was so ridiculous that we found ourselves laughing helplessly in this small break among the clouds of our grief.

Attending the funeral of your own child is something no parent ever expects to do, and it is grim. Pa had told me he was going to wear a white tie because when he was in India, it was the custom to wear white at the funerals of children. So I emulated him and wore a white dress. One of our friends hugged me afterwards and said, 'Well done for wearing white.' Before leaving us that day, my father asked if I had a photograph of William for him to see, so I took him upstairs to show him. We looked at it and hugged each other and cried, and then he said to me, 'You know, you will be happy again.' And I said to him, 'You are a lovely man, Daddy, I love you so much.' And we hugged again and dried our tears and went downstairs. And he was right.

Just over one year later, I gave birth to another baby boy, Alistair, who, as the years went by, became a constant source of pride and delight to his grandfather. Of course Alistair's arrival gave us another opportunity to see Cuthbert – as nobody else would do for his christening. This time, Cuthbert arranged with the incumbent vicar at Christ Church in Shamley Green to be permitted to officiate there, and was delighted to be back in the church where he had spent so many happy years. Clad in a white suit reminiscent of Andy Pandy, Alistair accepted the baptism of the Christian church with as good grace as his sister, regarding us with a puzzled expression as the holy water was poured over his little head.

As a very little boy, my father taught him to say, 'My dear fellow!' and this was their greeting to each other right up until the end of my father's life. Many a happy visit was made to my old childhood home as the children grew up and, on arrival, Hattie and Alistair would observe polite protocol for a few moments before asking my father, 'Can we draw in your studio?' All would have been made ready for them – paper, pens, paints and brushes – and the children would create for hours in the wonderland of an artist's studio while we grown-ups, under the gentle influence of wine and sunshine, would put the world to rights.

My father always felt that children are able to do more in art than we perhaps give them credit for, readily adapting to a method of producing a design that we might consider to be outside their abilities. It is after the age of around eight that children can become self-conscious about their ability to create a picture or a design –

but prior to that, a child will make a piece of artwork with no inhibitions. A young child will also adapt a creation they have made to suit their mood. At the age of five, I produced a drawing of a pin man with a round thing at the end of one of the stick arms and a long thing at the end of the other. Pa asked me what my character was holding. I informed him that the girl, for so it was, was holding a plate in one hand and a knife in the other. Asked the same question the next day, it transpired that the round thing was my character's hand and the long thing had become a ruler. Amazing. When faced with something totally unidentifiable drawn by a young person, Pa would always say, 'Tell me about this', instantly inviting a detailed and imaginative account of the masterpiece in question. Children's drawings of people often show them with huge hands – particularly when the drawing is a portrait of a grandmother. This, my father explained, is because generally the first thing a grandmother will do when she sees her grandchild is to put out her arms for a cuddle, so the lasting impression on the child of the grandmother is of vast hands reaching towards them.

In the main, life for my parents at the cottage in Shamley Green was a peaceful affair, a continuing round of frenzied work punctuated by short periods of rest in warm and sunny climes, games of croquet on the lawn at the cottage with the grandchildren, frequent lunch parties for work colleagues, film units, interested visitors, old friends and family.

Neighbours, too, played an important part, and when Rick and Annie Craig-Wood came to live in the house just behind the cottage, pleasant neighbourliness bloomed into a life-long friendship. Rick, whose accomplishments were many, flew a helicopter, and took my parents up to give them a bird's eye view of their house and the land around – a trip which gave my father a real thrill and which he often spoke about with delight. While they did not spend all their time in each other's pockets, a ritual was established shortly after Rick and Annie arrived and which continued year after year. Every Boxing Day, my father made his curry out of the leftover Christmas turkey for the family with its usual accompaniments – dhal, rice, vegetable curry and a small dish of hot sauce – and shortly after their arrival he invited Rick and Annie to join us. From then on, bearing bottles of champagne, the Craig-Woods would arrive each Boxing Day at lunchtime to join three generations of the Hart family and eat great plates of curry with gusto. Rick, who seemed to take a delight in everything and particularly his food, didn't turn a hair when one year one of my children managed to throw up immediately behind his chair. Having satisfied himself that the exploding child was all right and the carpet unlikely to have suffered permanent damage, he returned his benign attention to his plate, his glass and the assembled company.

My father's inner light shines through always. In his consideration towards others, in his own spirituality and in his unconditional love for those he holds dear. In his working life at the BBC there was never one person who was not happy to be working on his programmes – everyone was only too pleased to be involved. And this wasn't just because of my father's artistic capabilities, but also because of the way he was – polite and gentle always, but also caring, spiritual, sometimes childish, always kind, deeply emotional and wise.

GLITTERING PRIZES

Using pen and ink, Tony draws a detailed and atmospheric cartoon of a man in a Paris street striking a match to light his pipe. But this is not just any man, this is a cartoon of the French detective Maigret, played by Rupert Davies, who famously struck his match against a wall while Ron Grainer's haunting theme music played. Having won a BAFTA for his role as Maigret in 1961, Tony draws Rupert striking his match on his BAFTA award – never thinking for a moment that 37 years later, he would receive a BAFTA of his own.

The award-winning *Vision On* had contained very little speech, but *Take Hart* not only included interaction with the animated capers of Morph, but also scripted dialogue with Colin Bennett – the caretaker of Tony's Take Hart studio. Mr Bennett had been deliberately introduced into the programme's format in a bid to attract more boys among the viewers. Looking at the viewing figures, producer Christopher Pilkington had seen that the majority of young people watching *Take Hart* were girls, so he had decided to introduce a character who would ask the kind of questions that a boy might ask Tony – 'What do you really do for a living?' being one of the more unforgettable ones. Mr Bennett represented the section of the audience who perhaps did not quite understand where my father was coming from, but who had to be made to side with Tony and identify with his exasperation over Mr Bennett who could be so obtuse. Morph, of course, appealed to everybody, and the boys could laugh at Mr Bennett's incomprehension of Tony's relationship with Morph – the little Plasticine character who Mr Bennett could not see – and at the same time enjoy the pictures my father was making.

But my father found learning the scripted dialogue with Mr Bennett difficult, and I remember him at home throwing the script aside in exasperation saying, 'But I'm not an actor!' My mother and I would tell him that he acted his scenes with Mr Bennett very well indeed; my mother would also remind him of all the acting that he had done at school and with the Country Players in Maidstone. 'That was different,' he grumbled. 'No it wasn't,' replied my mother, and Pa would look at me and grin sheepishly – although at the time I didn't realise what a worry it actually was for him.

While my father thought highly of Colin, there was an element of anarchic comedy scripted into the programme with Mr Bennett's involvement that he found quite difficult to accept. While it contrasted well with Pa's gentle, laid-back style, my father could not wholeheartedly appreciate the slapstick comedy which on occasion resulted in the destruction of some of his art – although Colin himself felt that without the comic element the programme would have come off as too staid. My father would spend hours learning his words, and if Colin did not give him the exact cue word for his next bit of dialogue, the whole thing would grind to a halt. A trained actor, Colin would sometimes improvise or paraphrase his lines and this clashed horribly with my father's need to have everything rehearsed and nailed down with nothing left to chance. Pa did have good comic timing, however, and he developed a deadpan look that said, 'Do we really have to do this?' which could reduce Colin into fits of giggles.

'Watch out for that bucket, Mr Bennett! Too late.'

It wasn't until many years after making these programmes with my father that Colin acquired a slight sense of guilt – not in any way related to his contribution to the programme. This was because at the time he was working as an actor in London's West End, and in order to get to the theatre on time, all of Colin's scenes would be rehearsed and recorded first so that he could leave early. It dawned on him years later that the first part of the studio day must have been hugely pressured for my father as he and Pa got their scripted nonsense out of the way, and it was only after Colin had taken himself off to the theatre that Pa could settle down and concentrate on the artistic side of things.

But they did get on well together and, although both of them were highly professional and disciplined in their work, Colin could cause my Pa to collapse in a fit of giggles with a single look. Colin remembers an occasion when he was halfway up the spiral staircase that made up part of my father's studio set, dropping sycamore seed 'whirlybirds' on to my father below. This was all part of the script, but the pair of them had collapsed in uncontrollable giggles, and the more irritated producer Christopher Pilkington got, the worse the giggles became. With my father being completely unable to give the link to introduce the next section of the programme on account of laughing, Christopher eventually gave up and simply cut to an animated item. On another occasion, when Pa and Mr Bennett had been waiting on set for some time ready to record one of their items, the giggles set in again. Eventually the control gallery was ready to record, and when the floor manager asked if they were both ready they could only gasp out amid howls of laughter that they had been, but they weren't any more.

It was during the making of these programmes that a personal tragedy befell Colin – his six-year-old daughter died after a nine-month battle with leukemia. I remember Pa having the most enormous respect and admiration for Colin as he carried on clowning as the irrepressible Mr Bennett during this terrible time. Christopher Pilkington told me that my father stepped back from his own concerns at this time, and was warm and loving and generous. Colin remembers saying to my father that he believed he would never laugh again – and he remembers the truism of my father's reply: 'Yes, you will.'

Theirs was a polite friendship, which was in keeping with my father who was, as Colin put it, respectable, straight, upright and nice. Colin likes to think, however, that there was a tiny part of Pa that would have wanted to cut off his ear and starve in a garret, or throw a hissy fit and be a proper diva – but of course he was far too polite for any of that. It did, however, amuse both of them hugely to learn that letters had been sent in to the programme suggesting that my father and Colin were living together in the studio in a gay partnership.

Sometimes Mr Bennett could be extremely funny quite inadvertently. On one occasion, they were filming at a working farm for a *Take Hart* programme with the title of 'Down on the Farm', and for some reason to do with the storyline, Mr Bennett had attempted to disguise himself as a bird and had attached a ridiculous beak to his face. They had taken a break in filming, and were leaning against a fence talking idly, waiting for the next shot to be set up, when the farmer's wife came up to see how the filming was going. She peered at Colin's face adorned with its beak and turned to my father, asking anxiously, 'Has he done something to his nose?'

Needless to say, his reply would have been polite. Manners and politeness were hugely important to my father, and he brought me up to share the same values. 'Always be of service,' he told me, 'but never be servile.' He taught me the basic rules of table manners – and how to break them. This was important, as he would from time to time take me to lunch meetings at restaurants in London when I was as young as five or six years old (which now I stop to think about it was presumably because the current au pair was rendered *hors de combat*). He showed me how, when presented with a bowl of soup and a bread roll, to tilt the bowl and spoon the soup from the back of it, and to swirl it gently in the spoon for a moment if it was too hot – not to blow on it and risk blowing it off the spoon and splattering it over the table and adjacent diners. He showed me how to break pieces of bread from the roll and eat them – not to pick up the whole thing to take bites out of it. He made me roar with laughter by giving an impression of how not to eat soup, crouching over his bowl and dabbing a great lump of bread in it several times, then eating it with much slurping and dribbling. He did, however, show me that it was perfectly in order to dip pieces of bread into a soup bowl, or to wipe up sauce from a plate, provided it was done neatly, cleanly and with panache. A quick artistic bread-wipe design made in the remains of any gravy left on a plate was also acceptable – but only among friends.

Before we went out, he would look me over, checking that my hair was neat and tidy and my hands were clean. Recently home from school on one occasion, there was ink under my fingernails. 'Get rid of that,' he told me. 'But it's ink!' I protested. 'Get rid of it,' he insisted gently. With the aid of a nailbrush and much scrubbing I did manage to get rid of almost all of the offending ink – enough anyway to pass muster and to be taken up to London to attend another business lunch. What was talked about, I have no idea. I would be concentrating on my table manners, and responding politely to kindly words from my father's colleagues. I do, however, remember being in a fever of excitement at The Gun Room, a restaurant in the West End, because in the cellar was a cat who had just had kittens, and I was to be allowed to see them once I had finished my lunch – much more exciting than grown-up business conversation.

My father lost his temper once every seven years – or thereabouts. I remember him losing it with me just once when I was six. I had a sandpit in the garden, and Pa had been carefully sweeping all the sand that had escaped onto the grass back into the sandpit – a tedious and time-consuming job. Wanting to keep him company, I played in the sandpit while the cleanup operation was in progress – unaware that I was happily hurling the sand straight back out onto the grass. He was furious.

But when you are known for your even temper and good nature, it is all the more impressive on the rare occasions when you do completely blow your stack. Such was the case when Tony was recording one of his *Take Hart* programmes in Bristol. The item had not been going as well as it might, and it had had to be redone more than once already. Added to this, there were a number of visitors – mainly friends and family of the crew – watching in the studio which, as a rule, my father didn't mind at all, but on this particular day there were so many of them that he found he couldn't see the floor manager giving him his cues through the crush of people. Unable to give the job the concentration it needed, something inside suddenly snapped and my father yelled at the floor manager to get the people out of there. There was a moment's appalled silence during which you could have heard a pin drop, then everybody rushed to clear the studio, and my father was asked if he wanted to take a break, or if there was anything he wanted, anything at all, before carrying on.

I know Pa regretted his outburst, which he considered nothing less than rude, and he worried that those people who were in the studio that day must have thought him difficult and temperamental. But under those circumstances a lesser man would have thrown a hissy fit much earlier – and rightly so.

Over the years, my father worked with many cameramen, floor managers, directors and producers. Floor manager Cliff White worked with my father not only on *Vision On*, *Take Hart* and *Hart Beat*, but for the very first time on *Playbox* back in the fifties when he was a trainee cameraman. The job of a floor manager is to run the studio floor and to be the link between the director in the studio gallery and the artistes. A floor manager therefore needs to have the authority to demand and get instant silence from everybody in the studio when required, must be both friend and psychologist to his artistes, and must also have brilliant powers of diplomacy. For example, a stressed director, who can be heard only by the floor manager and the cameramen through their headphones, who wants a plump artiste to terminate her conversation with a colleague and move swiftly across the studio floor to a sofa on the set might yell something like, 'Get that fat cow off her arse and into the sofa area now!' Any floor manager worth his salt will translate this request into something like, 'Darling, we're ready to shoot in the sofa area now, so shall we?'

Cliff, of course, never needed to use any such powers of diplomacy where my father was concerned. Being such a gentle and polite man himself, any instructions from the director in the gallery would also be politely and kindly given. All of my father's programmes were made using a rehearse/record manner – in other words, Pa would run through what he was going to do two or three times so that the cameras could see where they needed to be, and then they would record the item. After that, they would rehearse the next item, and then record it – and so on through the day. Everything that had been recorded would then be edited together later to give the finished programme.

While Pa was pretty relaxed during the rehearsals he would, however, become quite tense just before the recording. Cliff found a way of dealing with this. Just before they started to record an item, on an instruction from Christopher Pilkington in the gallery and using a funny voice, Cliff would say, 'Shoulders'. The effect of this was twofold – as my father became more tense, his shoulders would begin to rise, but as soon as Cliff said 'Shoulders' he would immediately drop them – and the funny voice would make him smile and relax, as it is of course quite impossible to be tense when you are smiling.

Cliff also had a saying that became something of a catchphrase and never failed to make Pa chuckle. Quiet is demanded on any studio floor, but especially so for my father's programmes. This was because my father would be quietly talking about what he was doing as he was making his pictures, so absolute silence was necessary when they were recording. It would get pretty hot under the studio lights, and to counter this there would be fans roaring away during the rehearsal periods to keep the studio as cool as possible, and these would be switched off just before recording. And in order to prevent anyone barging into the studio during the recording and making a noise, a red light would go on above the studio doors. So when an item had been rehearsed to everybody's satisfaction and all was ready to go for a recording, Cliff would say, 'Red lights and fans, please' – meaning red lights on and fans off, but of course all sorts of interpretations could be put on this phrase – an exotic dancer in a nightclub springs to my mind – and it was the thought of what mental images those around him were conjuring up from Cliff's words that made my father smile.

Cliff and my father got on very well together – both sharing the same fondness for whimsical humour – and when Pa was diagnosed with diabetes, Cliff would keep a close eye on him and engineer short breaks during the studio day so that Pa could take himself off and rejuvenate his flagging sugar levels with a biscuit.

The animated adventures of Morph would be recorded in advance of my father's programme – with David Sproxton and Peter Lord bringing the tape themselves to the studio – so Pa would be able to see what Morph was up to and react accordingly. David and Peter would also bring Morph's pencil box with them because for continuity purposes it had to be the same box that appeared in both my father's studio set and in the animated films. If the script required dialogue between my father and Morph, Pa would have to look at specific points on his table, holding a conversation with thin air – this one-way conversation would come to life in the magic of editing afterwards. When Morph appeared to be throwing paint at my father, it was Cliff who would invariably be flicking paint at my father's face on behalf of his troublesome Plasticine companion. He never missed.

Take Hart ran for ten years, and at the end of it the programme was nominated for, and won, a BAFTA award. Tony was invited to the ceremony in 1984, but my mother was not and, although thrilled at being nominated, my father refused to go without her. So his producer, Christopher Pilkington, collected the award on his behalf while he and my mother watched the ceremony on television at home. There were, however, many subsequent awards ceremonies and glittering occasions to which my mother was invited along with my father – including another BAFTA presentation 14 years later, this time a lifetime achievement award.

In the meantime, I had been working as a production secretary on the BBC's *Multi-Coloured Swap Shop*, a live three-hour Saturday morning children's programme with, at the end of each series, an awards programme of our own, with nominations voted for by our viewers. In 1979 Pa was proving popular in the Favourite TV Personality category, and it was fun to pop down to the large dressing room that had been commandeered for sorting and counting all the letters and postcards to see how he was doing. 'He's doing okay!' I would be told, and shooed out. He was doing very okay, because he was one of the three top nominees for that category (the other two were Lesley Judd and Tom Baker) and therefore had to come and attend our sparkling awards ceremony. My mother and father arrived at the BBC's Television Centre and, with my mother at the wheel, took their car into the multistorey car park. Their car was big, and the spaces in the car park were tight. With another car revving impatiently behind them, my mother was carefully trying to reverse into a space and making a botch of it. When the waiting car leaned on its horn, my dinner-jacketed father got out and went over to the impatient female driver. With a gentle smile he told her, 'You're not helping.' She stared back at him and then, covering her face with her hands, burst out 'I'm sorry!' Given the same set of circumstances, many of us would have marched over to the impatient vehicle demanding, 'What's your problem then?' Not my darling dad – who later that evening – and indeed again the following year – found himself the winner of *Swap Shop's* Favourite TV Personality award.

There was a bitter-sweetness, however, to the winning of the *Take Hart* BAFTA award. The viewing figures for series nine and ten were beginning to drop. Christopher Pilkington researched this and talked to many people and was told by some that they didn't watch the programme any more because 'they knew it'. He decided it was time to find a new format with a new title, and to find a way of injecting a new and different energy – but to do it without disturbing the heart of the show (the pun, he told me, fully intended).

Christopher travelled the British Isles looking for another Tony Hart – somebody who could appear alongside the original and introduce new techniques and ideas, but despite visiting every art college in the country, he was unable to find someone who could match my father's amazing versatility and appeal. He did, however, find four art students who, although collectively still did not quite equal my father's ability, could individually inject a new colour and flavour into the new show, entitled *Hart Beat*. The new format had been discussed and my father had met the girls but, while outwardly appearing to be enthusiastically championing the idea, inwardly he was not happy – over the years each new addition to his programme had meant that he was having to let go a little bit, a hard thing to do having been a solo performer for some time.

At the Grosvenor House Hotel, immediately after Christopher had accepted the BAFTA for *Take Hart*, he went straight to a telephone to speak to my father and tell him the great news. Both my parents were absolutely thrilled, but after expressing his delight the next thing Pa said to Christopher was, 'Does this mean we don't have to do the new show?' – believing that if the original format had won the award, then surely there was no need to change it. Christopher, inwardly weeping for my dad, took a deep breath and told him, 'Yes we do. We need to move forward in order to capture a bigger audience, and play with some new toys.' My father never mentioned it again, and embraced the new show unreservedly.

Hart Beat started in 1985 and followed a similar format to *Take Hart* with Morph and Chas continuing to cause trouble, and Mr Bennett providing the slapstick comedy, but now there was the addition of a quartet of attractive young ladies who each had their own area of expertise, bringing new techniques and ideas to the new show. Margot Wilson made models out of card, and her work was clean and sharp and defined; Jo Kirk was about mess, producing big, wild paintings, which contrasted with my father's clean lines; Liza Brown's background was in fashion design, and she worked with fabric and textiles; and Gabrielle Bradshaw specialised in metal sculpture, and was often to be seen wearing an eye shield and wielding a blowtorch to create something spectacular out of remnants from a breaker's yard. A good-looking girl, on one occasion Gabrielle hid her attractive features behind a false moustache for an item for *Hart Beat*. Dressed in costumes reminiscent of black-and-white movie icons Stan Laurel and Oliver Hardy, she and my father took it in turns to peel away pieces from a black-and-white church window design of a choirboy, revealing a section of bright colour underneath. Speeded up like the old silent movies, and accompanied by appropriate comic piano music, they gave each other the thumbs up as each black or white piece was peeled away until eventually the brilliant colours of a glorious stained glass window were fully revealed. Very pleased with themselves, the pair linked arms and wobbled their way off.

Years later Gabrielle wrote to me:

'I often wondered what Tony thought of us all and how he truly felt about sharing his programme with four girls fresh from art college with no prior TV experience. Whatever his true feelings, he was of course an absolute gentleman and gave us all the help and encouragement he could, allowing us not only to shine in his light but also to learn at the pencil tip of the master!'

Before the start of the series, all four girls went to the cottage with producer Christopher Pilkington to meet my father and have lunch. Knowing Pa's true feelings about the new format, Christopher told me that both my father and my mother were warm and welcoming and wonderful hosts to the girls that day – and that the girls were utterly terrified at the prospect of meeting my Pa who they themselves considered an icon. But they were soon put at their ease and when Pa took them out to the studio and they saw the enormous amount of preparation work that was in hand for the new series, one or two of them were seriously shocked. Without putting it into words, my father demonstrated to them that in a television studio, time was money, and proper preparation was essential.

After the girls had gone, Christopher stayed behind and told my dad what a marvellous man he was. Despite his own reservations about the new programme, my father had taken the high ground, engaging and welcoming and motivating the girls, and they in turn had been blown away by him.

It seems everyone thought a lot of my darling dad. When Christopher moved on to produce other shows, he was very careful about finding his own replacement, and felt that the young Chris Tandy was the only person who would properly look after the treasure that Pa was.

Chris Tandy was at the same time both delighted and anxious

about taking up the *Hart Beat* reins – wondering what my father would think about this young whippersnapper coming in to take control of his programme. He need not have worried, as my father instantly took to his new producer – and Chris similarly found Pa a delight to work with. He remembers the studio days as being great fun, principally because of my father's enormous enthusiasm for what he was doing and everybody's sheer enjoyment at being involved with his wonderful designs. He found my father to be the perfect artiste –always on time, always prepared and, having built up such a good understanding of television over the years, able to take direction easily – always knowing exactly why a thing had to be repeated or filmed in a particular way. If a design did not turn out on camera as well as he had hoped, my father would explain the effect he was trying to achieve, and would then allow the director and the camera crew to find a way of accomplishing it. Sometimes there would be some interaction with the girls or Mr Bennett, or the scripting of a link that my Pa was not entirely comfortable with. Chris remembers that he would never refuse to do any of these, but he had a way of suddenly going very quiet – which Chris soon learned to recognise meant my father was not happy, and that he needed to find another way of doing things.

It was important that my father's producers knew and understood him well. He would never say no to anything, and would sometimes even say an enthusiastic 'yes' when in fact he did not entirely agree with what was being proposed. Christopher Pilkington said that with my dad, you had to learn to tell when 'yes' meant 'yes', and when 'yes' meant 'no'!

Chris Tandy was my father's third producer in a 30-year period of programme making, and while the creation of the designs and pictures remained as popular as ever, Chris felt his brief was to find a way to embellish Pa's concepts with contemporary settings, graphics and music so that the programme remained fresh.

Among the regular items, Tony would produce a picture that took four minutes to complete, and this section came to be known as 'Tony's four-minuters'. As they started, it was impossible to tell what the picture was going to be. One of these began with a few geometric shapes made with a thick black marker pen towards the top of a sheet of grey paper, then white chalk was scribbled over them and smoothed over with cotton wool. This made the black pen and background appear much paler. Moving down the sheet of paper, Pa would repeat the exercise, drawing more geometric shapes and one or two sloping contours with the black marker pen. Then he repeated the white chalk scribble – but less of it this time. A wipe with cotton wool, and this section of the picture was pale, but not as pale as the first section. The black marker pen was used once more to make more shapes; orange chalk added a bit of brighter detail here and there, and several wiggly vertical lines of grey chalk, smudged with a finger, ran from some of the geometric shapes to the top of the picture – and there before you, with smoke pouring from the chimneys, was a rooftop landscape fading away into the distance. The swiftly drawn addition of a black figure holding a chimney sweep's brush completed the effect.

My father's programmes were bursting not only with different ways to make pictures or models or sculptures, but also with bits of interesting information. While displaying a selection of shepherd's crooks, we learned that the curved section at the top was made from horn, which must be heated in order to be bent into shape before being carved into the most wonderfully intricate designs. In another programme we learned that 16th-century gold coins recovered from the sunken ship *Mary Rose* were called 'angels' because of the image of Archangel Michael that appeared on one side. In one of his programmes for younger viewers we learned what different animals' tails are used for – a defence mechanism for whisking away insects in the case of a horse, a warning signal for rabbits and a balancing aid-cum-parachute for squirrels.

And this enthusiastic, gentle way he used to impart information in his television programmes was exactly the way in which he imparted useful information about life, the world and everything to me at home.

Another way of making a picture of petrified trees in a swamp or a winter woodland scene for *Hart Beat* was created out of a game played with Margot. By dropping a few blobs of ink on to a piece of paper, and then blowing at it carefully through a straw, Tony and Margot would blow at the ink, causing it to run in different directions like the branches of a tree. Satisfied with the effect they had achieved with the ink, Tony would, with a sweep of a brush, anchor the trees to the ground, and, with a few strokes of a fibre-tip pen, add a fence, while a final squiggle placed a bird on the stump of a dead tree. My father's programmes were full of fantastic and sometimes unlikely ways to make a picture, all meticulously tried and tested before committing them to film. A true professional, he was always extremely well prepared and rehearsed. And when all the designs were done he would always finish each programme with a smile and the same words – 'See you next time.'

Something of a marathon was my father's artwork that accompanied the composer Saint-Saëns's *Carnival of the Animals* – not for television this, but a party piece of his when entertaining large crowds. *Carnival of the Animals* is a piece of music that lasts for 22 minutes and has 14 movements, each describing an animal – perfect for drawing to. So, with an expectant crowd ready and a vast piece of paper measuring seven-and-a-half square metres in position, the music would start and Pa's marker pen would begin to whiz around in a series of squiggles and slashes all across the paper. Then, working around a particular squiggle or slash, a lion with crown and flowing mane would be revealed. As the music changed, a strutting cockerel would rapidly appear, followed by a dancing elephant, a kangaroo, several fish, a donkey, birds – on and on it would go until, 20 minutes later, with his hand trembling with fatigue, Pa would complete the last creature – a swan. This enormous artwork produced at high speed was a world away from the calm images he produced in the studio, and although hugely entertaining was also utterly exhausting – Pa would say that by the time the music reached its finale, he was pretty much finished, too.

Another piece of artwork that hangs in my cousin Simon's house to this day had a very different inspiration from the piece by Saint-Saëns. In 1969 brother Michael succumbed to a nasty case of haemorrhoids and was briefly hospitalized to remedy this uncomfortable condition. Full of sympathy, Pa created a large and colourful abstract artwork to cheer him. An art critic might describe this piece as a complex of feelings, a tumult of reds and browns and tumescent pinks rendered asunder with vast shapes of a lighter hue, buffeting and drawing one into a dark crevice where pain and serenity combine. Its inspiration? Michael's piles.

Over the years, Tony produced many specially commissioned drawings and designed many logos. Payment didn't always come into it – and sometimes even when it did, it wasn't in money. When I was working on the *Multi-Coloured Swap Shop*, Noel Edmonds's first wife had just acquired her private pilot's licence. Noel asked me if I would ask Pa if he could do a cartoon of Gill to mark the event. He gave me a photograph for my father to work from, and Pa came up with a glorious cartoon of this very glamorous lady in a flying hat and jacket holding up a compact mirror and putting on her lipstick, while in the background, a little aeroplane was skywriting 'Congratulations Biggles!'. On delivery, Noel asked me what the cost was for the drawing. I relayed the question to Pa who wrote out an invoice: 'To one Biggles cartoon – one bottle of plonk', which I duly passed to

Noel. Nothing happened for a few days, and then one afternoon there was the sound of wheels crunching on the gravel drive, and a car drew up. It was Noel's driver who had come to deliver not a bottle but a case of very lovely wine.

A few years later, an old friend in the shape of cricketing commentator Brian Johnston telephoned my father to tell him that Sir Paul Getty, another close friend of his, had built a cricket pitch. He wanted a logo for his Wormsley cricket team and had asked if he knew anybody who might be able to help. Brian, who had known my father since *Ask Your Dad* days, told him he had a friend who could draw a bit, and Mr G (as he was called) asked him to ask my father to come up with a suggestion. Tony considered the name – 'worm' could also mean dragon, and 'lee' which could mean couch or bed. So he came up with a dragon that was halfway between a heraldic beast and a cartoon sitting on a stylised couch holding a cricket bat. Mr G was delighted with it, and the logo adorned the fixtures correspondence and the flag that flew over the pavilion. As this had been a favour for a friend, there was no talk of payment. But a few days later, there was another scrunching of wheels on gravel, and this time it was Mr G's driver who had come to deliver a case of exceptionally beautiful champagne.

Then came another call from Brian Johnston. Mr G would like the logo to appear on a tie for his club – did my father know anybody who might be able to help? By this time, I had left the BBC and was working for a company that designed and produced corporate neckwear, so Pa replied that he thought he knew somebody who might be able to help in this regard. So we designed a classic tie in woven silk in the green and gold colours of the club, which we saw being worn by the members whenever we were invited to attend one of their summer fixtures. It was on one of these occasions, a glorious gentle day spent in a deck chair sitting around a perfect cricket pitch nestled in the Chilterns, punctuated by lunch in a flower-filled marquee, that my father found himself sitting next to one of the players. Pouring white wine for everyone at the table, Tony offered the cricketer a glass, but he refused saying that he was due to go out to bat after lunch. Tasting the wine, my father implored him, 'Oh, but you must try a little, it is so good!' 'Alright,' replied the cricketer, 'but just one glass.' After lunch, he went out and promptly scored a century. When he was finally out, he came and found my father and announced, 'From now on, I shall always have one glass of wine before I go out to bat!'

During the making of his television programmes, my father had a brief brush with the world of commercial advertising and was asked to make two advertisements. This was never entirely straightforward because at that time it was only permissible for BBC contracted artistes to appear in a commercial provided that the advert did not over-emulate the programme in which the artiste appeared. Both of the commercials alluded to my father's area of expertise but were considered to be far enough away in concept from his programmes, and so were allowed. One of these was a whacky ad for Ambrosia Creamed Rice where he was apparently seeking a drawing to communicate the creaminess of the rice – aptly choosing a line drawing of the rear end of a cow in preference to the Mona Lisa and a drawing of a tennis racquet.

He enjoyed doing this one, but he found an earlier advert for a manufacturer of kitchen appliances very difficult indeed. Bearing in mind he would make one complete programme in a single day, he found the two days it took to make a 30-second commercial infinitely more stressful. The concept, however, was nice. He was to make a speedy design of square geometric shapes in white string on a big black wall, which included a long horizontal line of string running close to the ground interrupted by a small angular shape. The string was held in place by black drawing pins, invisible to the camera against the black background. Rapidly taking the string around the pins to make the design, my father caught his thumb on one of them and it started to bleed, staining the pristine white string. Everything had to stop, more string had to be fetched, and Pa's finger had to be invisibly sealed before they could carry on. My poor father was made to feel rather guilty about causing this hitch in the proceedings so, being very careful not to bleed, he had another go. This time all went well, with the speedy completion of the string outline. With the magic of editing afterwards, the geometric shapes gently morphed into cupboards and appliances in a warm, glowing kitchen while the small angular shape near to the floor became a white wagging tail. The last shot of the advertisement was of Pa scooping a small West Highland terrier out of one of the low level kitchen cupboards into his arms and saying, 'How did you get in there?' It was a nice concept, and I'm sure the money was nice too – but it was not one of my father's more enjoyable television experiences.

In 1990 at the age of 65, my father was delighted and immensely proud to be invited to speak to the Oxford Union, the world-renowned debating society open to all the students from all the Oxford colleges. He was thrilled to join the ranks of speakers that included world leaders, rock stars, cabinet ministers, film stars – even Kermit the Frog. In the audience to see him, jammed in among the graduates, undergraduates and fellows from all the disciplines of all the colleges was Susie Ross, my husband's niece and at that time a student at Oxford, studying medicine. She told me that my father entertained a packed chamber with stories and jokes before starting to draw in response to the students' vociferous and enthusiastic requests. There were elephants, she remembers, and tigers, and Morph was certainly in evidence, and at the end of it all the drawings were auctioned to raise money for the Gurkha Welfare Trust. 'Everybody loved it,' Susie told me. 'he was from our era – it was like being ten again!'

But the glory of my dad is that he was from so many people's eras, with the ability to make not only the 20-year-olds but also the 30-year-olds, the 40-year-olds, and even the 50-year-olds feel ten again.

Four years after his appearance at the Oxford Union, my father embarked on making a new series for the BBC at Hillside Studios in Bushey entitled *The Artbox Bunch*. Produced by his old friend Chris Tandy, this show was more simplistic in style than *Hart Beat* or *Take Hart* and was aimed at younger viewers. While Pa demonstrated how to draw and colour a frog or a duck, or produce a template to give an image of the Houses of Parliament, a bunch of animated drawing accoutrements appeared alongside him and spent their time being not terribly nice to each other. A bespectacled ruler and rubber, a glue stick, pens, pencils, a sharpener, scissors and a set of compasses, all sporting expressive little faces and who all lived together in the eponymous large wooden art box, spent their time trying to blow each other up, knock each other down or chuck each other into water. It was CMTB Animations who produced these animated inserts – not Aardman, who were responsible for Morph – and rather than shooting on 16mm film, they shot their images directly onto video tape in a studio which had been rigged with lighting to match that of the live-action studio. This meant that the animated pictures could be integrated far more convincingly with the studio images, and a shot of my father with one of the *Art Box Bunch* characters on his desk could be edited seamlessly with the animated sequence.

The technology was clever, but to my mind the characters of the *Art Box Bunch* lacked the charm of Morph and, even though the animated sequences were so much more cleverly integrated with the live action, the characters seemed somehow a little disconnected from what Pa was doing. But the show did well, running for two series on terrestrial television before being repeated on the digital channels, and my father liked Hillside which had originally been built by the Rank Organisation – a firm of devout Quakers who had stipulated that a proportion of the programmes made there had a religious content. Perhaps something of the spiritual nature of those shows lingered in the studio, making itself felt as Pa worked on his own programmes.

It was while my father was making *The Art Box Bunch* programmes that my marriage collapsed after 21 years. At Will's insistence, I rang my father. As always, he answered the phone singing the number and, as always, I said 'Papa!' and our conversation would continue with him asking me how I was. This time, instead of replying 'Fine!' I said hesitantly, 'Not so good.' 'Home or work?' he asked. 'Home.' I replied. 'Oh dear,' he said, 'oh dear, oh dear. Want to come down?' 'Yes please,' I said, feeling about twelve. So down I went. We sat out in the garden in the sunshine and had lunch, and I told my mother and father all about what had gone wrong with my marriage, and how I had managed to get myself tangled up in an unhealthy obsessive relationship with somebody else. They let me talk and made no judgemental remarks, asking only if I thought it might be a bad patch. After a while, my mother went inside to make some coffee, and my father quietly confessed to an affair he had had long ago and which had lasted for two years. He told me that it had been exciting and wonderful for the first six months, but then the relationship had limped on for another eighteen while he tried to find a kind way to end it. Eventually the lady in question brought it all to a close herself, much to his relief. My mother reappeared with the coffee, and set the tray down on the table remarking, 'We went through a bad patch didn't we, for about two years.' Pa and I exchanged a glance, and never spoke of it again.

But bad patch or not, my marriage ended, and although it was probably one of the most amicable divorces of all time, it brought with it its own degree of stress and grieving that the death of any relationship brings, and through which my father's support was unstinting. It pleases me to add that through all the years that followed, although we were no longer married, my father continued to hold Will in the highest regard and was always delighted to see him whenever he went to visit.

It was at one of the Wormsley cricketing fixtures two or three years later that my second husband Ross (who, although his name is Martyn, has always been known by his surname since his schooldays) – who at that time I had not yet married and wasn't quite sure about – took my mother to one side and asked what he should do to win my affections. 'Don't ask me to interfere,' she replied. 'She won't take any notice of what I say to her.' Actually I would have done, but it was Pa who took me aside one day shortly afterwards and stated, 'You love him.' 'Do I?' I asked. 'Yes you do,' he said firmly. And that was that. And I do, very much.

By this time, my father was making a series of much shorter art programmes for the BBC titled *Smart Hart*, again produced by Chris Tandy, and co-presenting alongside Kirsten O'Brien. This time, these were filmed in his very own studio at the cottage where, with gentle fun, he instructed Kirsten on how to make pictures. The programmes also included the ever popular Morph and Chas, along with clips from *Hart Beat* and *Take Hart*. Following the format of all his previous series, each programme was based around a single theme.

In one of the programmes entitled 'Animals', he showed Kirsten how to draw a creature that was cute in style by starting off with two pencil squares, one above the other, then shaping an oval to make a head around the top square. Drawing a cross centrally through this oval gave the position of a nose swiftly followed by eyes and mouth, and then – remarking that once the ears are done, you can usually tell what the creature is – he finished off with his marker pen to reveal an appealing cat. Kirsten followed suit, producing a similar head and body shape, then adding a face and limbs, again leaving the ears until last to reveal her drawing of a teddy bear. It was a nice mixture, my father now aged 74 with his gentle charm and ubiquitous cravat – a small vanity that allowed him to cover signs of aging – and the young and bubbly Kirsten, each of them treating the other with respect and consideration and fun, but it was noticeable that Pa's drawing was not quite as confident as it had been in previous years. In a programme with the subject title of '3D', he showed Kirsten how to give depth and dimension to a drawing of a vase by deciding where the light source should be, and shading it accordingly. Using a charcoal pencil, Kirsten followed suit and, to my mind, produced the better drawing.

But my father's popularity continued unabated, and from time to time he appeared on other people's programmes. One of these was *Meet Ricky Gervais*, a chat show for Channel 4. Ricky's somewhat cocky style contrasted sharply with my father's gentle well-mannered charm, and I wondered if Pa would be able to hold his own. During the show, having commented that my father could make a picture out of anything, Ricky produced in succession a number of items including two plums and a banana asking, with a naughty smile, what he could make out of those. This was not a new one on Pa, who swiftly arranged the pieces of fruit to make – a smiley face.

Because of my father's charming and polite personality, coupled with the fact that he was a television presenter for children, some people would feel obliged to try to shock or embarrass him to see what he would do. But Pa had not only served as a Gurkha officer in India, he had also been around for a long time and was pretty unshockable. I think the only time that I rendered him momentarily speechless was when at the tender age of nine I informed him that I found the school subject of mathematics to be absolute crap. Believing that the word meant 'not much fun', I was completely nonplussed by my father, who was doing his best not to laugh while he told me that this was not perhaps the politest word I could have used.

A friend of ours told a Gurkha tale to my father that some might have thought he would have been shocked by – but he wasn't, and indeed the tale was a backhanded compliment. A group of friends and family, including my father who was wearing his Gurkha tie, and a friend and neighbour in the shape of one John Faulkener, attended an evening event with a military flavour at the beautiful Stowe school in Buckinghamshire. Seated on the grass around an arena in front of the South Face along with several hundred others, we took a picnic and ate and drank while we watched parachutists float down into the arena trailing smoke from canisters fitted to their ankles, as well as spectacular fireworks, and marching displays by several military bands, including the Band of the Brigade of Gurkhas. Watching these little men doing a fast march, John, happily lubricated with wine and waving a chicken leg, remarked to my father, 'Tough little bastards, these chaps.' 'Really,' replied my father, 'do you have some experience of this?' John told him that his father, who had been a dispatch rider in the RASC during the war, had run into a bunch of Gurkhas in London and got swept along marching nonstop from Waterloo to Staines to get, as John put it, the hell out of the Blitz. 'What did he think of them?' asked my father. 'All cock and knives.' replied John blandly. My father lifted an eyebrow as his hand went to his collar. 'You haven't recognised the tie!' he said. 'As a matter of fact I did,' replied John with a smile. 'That's why I told you the story!'

Another programme my father was invited to appear on was *Banzai*, a comedy gambling show that spoofed Japanese game shows. The programme was made up of bizarre contests on which the audience was frenziedly exhorted to place bets; it was totally ridiculous and my children and I enjoyed it enormously. People who went on the show, however, did tend to look pretty silly and I did wonder if it was a good idea for Pa to appear. The contest he took part in involved some rather elderly people dancing to silence in a nightclub environment, and my father had merely to stand swaying behind a DJ's table with one hand to his ear apparently mixing – which of course he had to be shown how to do. The contest was for the viewers to guess what music my Pa was playing for the old people to dance to – which turned out to be a track by Radiohead! The whole thing was completely bizarre, but it didn't do him any harm – if anything it made him look rather hip.

One morning, he called me to say that he had been asked to appear on *Esther* – a daily television show hosted by Esther Rantzen, this one being titled *Fame in the Family* - and would I appear on it with him? I replied that, of course, I would, and we talked for ages discussing what stories we thought we should tell. The format of the programme was to have several well-known parent and child combinations sitting in a panel in front of an audience that was made up of parents and children of more well-known people including the singer Joe Brown's daughter Sam, and the parents of pop singer Toyah Wilcox, and were interviewed by Esther on the subject of fame in the family.

While we waited in one of the green rooms at Television Centre, Pa and I, who hadn't seen each other for a few weeks, talked and talked – mainly about what was happening in my love-life at that time. Sitting across from us was the actor Nadim Sawalha who was appearing on the show as one of the panel with his daughter Julia. Nadim, who I shall adore forever for what he said, knew my father by sight, and came across to say hello and to ask who I was. 'This is my daughter!' replied my father proudly. 'I wondered if it was,' said Nadim, 'because the two of you were talking like friends.'

It was shortly after the *Smart Hart* series started that we noticed that my father always seemed to be dropping things – knives, forks and pencils. Whenever we visited, we would lay bets on how many times he would drop something – and then when he did we would treat it as a standing joke and cheer and clap every time it happened. With hindsight, we realised it must have been the early effects of some small strokes that he was having. One morning, Pa was making scrambled eggs for my mother, and as he took the pan from the cooker to the table and tried to put it down, he followed the pan and eggs down on to the floor. My mother heaved him up, and although he seemed to recover quickly – indeed, scrambling a new batch of eggs for their breakfast – she called the doctor, who recommended sending him for tests. These confirmed that he had indeed suffered one or two small strokes, but these appeared not to have caused any severe loss of mobility or dexterity. So Tony continued making his personal appearances with Roc, and although he was drawing very little, the appearances proved as popular as ever, and did him a world of good.

One of the Japanese car manufacturers booked him to do a series of appearances for their personnel in hotels all over the country. The employees spent the day attending seminars and lectures, and then gathered for drinks and dinner in the evening. At some point during the day, they had been supplied with paper and pens and asked to design a car. As dinner was drawing to a close, the background music stopped and the *Vision On* gallery theme began to play. Waiting outside the doors of the restaurant, my father could hear the people inside talking to each other saying, 'I know that music, what is it? It's *Vision On* – you know, Tony Hart.' Then the doors would open and, to their delight and amazement, in would come my tuxedo-clad father to judge their motor-car drawings. It went down very well. The car people loved it, but I think my father loved it even more.

Making another personal appearance at the opening of a new art shop some distance away, Tony and Roc stayed in a hotel overnight before making the journey home. They had their dinner accompanied by several glasses of wine and eventually took themselves off to bed in their respective rooms. Never one for pyjamas, Pa awoke in the night needing a pee. Groping his way to what he believed was the bathroom door, he stepped through it and out into the hotel corridor. Before his sleep-addled brain could assess the situation, the bedroom door closed behind him, locking him out with a soft click. Unembarrassed but a little disconcerted at finding himself stark naked in the corridor, Tony considered what to do. He toyed with the idea of striding boldly down to the lobby and asking assistance from the night porter, but on reflection decided it would be better to try and find some sort of garment before seeking help. He trotted off down the corridor, and found a janitor's cupboard. A quick rummage among the mops and buckets yielded a pair of orange waterproof trousers held up with braces. Clad in this fetching garment, Tony set off back down the corridor, this time in search of the night porter – who only a moment later he saw walking purposefully towards him. Delighted to have found help so quickly at hand, my father started to explain his predicament, indicating his attractive trousering. Without a flicker of expression, the night porter led the way back to my father's room, and opened the door for him. Acknowledging my father's effusive thanks with an unsmiling 'goodnight', he disappeared back in the direction from whence he had come. It was only later, when safely back in bed and thinking how lucky it was that the night porter had turned up when he did, that Tony stopped to consider the number of security cameras there were in the hotel corridors, and to wonder whether the night porter had enjoyed his impromptu naked one-man show.

WHERE SHADOWS FALL

To the plaintive sound of a plucked Spanish guitar, Tony smoothes a sheet of yellow paper with his hands. Using the side of his pastel crayons, he sweeps broad lines of red and brown across the top and bottom of the paper, leaving a round space near the top, which he fills with a solid circle of white pastel. With a tissue, he smudges the colours to create a hazy effect. Still using the white pastel crayon, he adds a scattering of shapes below – a shape like a triangle on its side, a few loops creating a cage-like effect, some smaller lines and dots – then adds a touch of black here and there. With a grey pastel crayon, he draws a few vertical lines randomly across the paper which he smudges with his finger, and then again adds a touch of black.   Finally, and again with his finger, he drags the black pastel from each vertical in a short line obliquely downwards, creating sharp dark shadows, and we recognise the sun-whitened bones of a cow lying in the shimmering heat of a desert where the skeletons of the dead trees point their mute message to the blistering sky.

I think it is true to say that my father lived a charmed life for 77 years. He grew up in a happy, loving environment, he loved his school in Dorset and his army years in India. He enjoyed college and then spent the rest of his life doing what he loved best as a profession, achieving a gentle fame and sufficient wealth to be comfortable. Along the way, he gathered many friends and a small family about him, which he loved more than anything else. It was only when tragedy struck one member of this little family that the rose-tinted hue of my father's existence waned and the shadows began to grow long.

For about two years before she died, my mother had complained of grumbling pains in her back and stomach. In trying to find out the cause of this, for months my poor mummy stoically endured just about every test imaginable, with chemicals poured up her, down her, and injected into her. But all the doctors would say was, 'We don't know what it is.'

Then, the day before Christmas Eve 2002, she had a stroke, which confined her to hospital for six weeks. My father had long since stopped driving and so I drove down every other day for that first week to take him to see her. Propped up on a heap of pillows, my mother was in good spirits but very much weakened down one side. The first time the family went to visit, Pa went and sat close beside her on the bed, laid his head on her shoulder and closed his eyes. Ross was with us, and I put a hand on his arm, gently drawing him away as it looked very much to me as if my parents wanted some time alone together.

Time passed in a routine of hospital visits – made hilarious by every member of the family, including the grandchildren, trying out her moving orthopaedic seat cushion, which would suddenly come to life, causing the current occupant to give an involuntary squeak of surprise – until eventually my mother came home. It was so good to see her there, albeit walking about carefully with a stick, or leaning on the work surfaces as she made her way cautiously around the kitchen.

June came and my father wanted to take her away to Italy as always, but she was worried about the trip and didn't think she was well enough to go. Knowing how much she loved Italy, I told her that although the journey would be pretty ghastly, it would be glorious once she was there. So she went, and although she could no longer walk up the hill to their favourite restaurant, she could be driven. She swam every day and, as it always had done, Italy's wonderful sunshine, food and wine worked its magic on their love life. After lunch one day, my father told me he arrived back at their room somewhat sweaty and out of breath having walked down the hill while my mother had been driven back to Le Agavi, to find her sitting serenely on their terrace. 'Are you terribly hot and tired, my darling?' she asked. 'No, no, not at all,' replied my father, trying not to pant. 'Want to play?' she suggested with a wicked smile. I don't think it would have mattered how hot and out of breath my Pa was – of course he wanted to play.

It was only a few weeks after they got back that Ross and I got married – twice. The first wedding was a quiet registry office affair in Richmond with just four friends and my two children, Hattie and Alistair, present; and the second was a blessing ceremony in a 17th-century Baptist meeting house in Winslow, followed by a big party in a friend's garden – John Faulkener's no less. My father came, but my mother did not, sending a card telling me that she was very wobbly on her legs and did not want to spoil things by falling over and making a fool of herself. My mother had always been elegant and dignified, so although desperately disappointed not to have her there, I understood. What I did not realise was how ill she had become. A week after the second wedding, Ross and I went away to France – bizarrely, to share our honeymoon with friends. Immediately on our return I rang my parents and Pa told me that my mother wasn't terribly well and that the doctor was with her, but we could come and visit in a day or two when she should be better.

Two days later, early in the morning, my father rang and said, 'Darling, you must prepare yourself for the worst – your mother has died.' I rushed down to the cottage, and there followed a flurry of contacting people and making arrangements in a state of shock and between sudden bouts of crying that would happen without warning. It was still summer and we spent all our time in my father's garden; it seemed to be easier to deal with everything there. I asked Pa if he and my mother had ever talked about what either of them wanted for their funerals – he told me they had never discussed it. But he had a very good idea of what he wanted for her – hymns, readings and prayers; he had it all sorted. The day of the funeral was a mixture of sorrow and happiness – and the party in the garden afterwards on that late August afternoon was full of sunshine and old friends, some of whom we hadn't seen for years.

At first my father seemed to bear up remarkably well, but my mother's death had been a terrible shock, and as autumn gave way to winter, Pa seemed to become less and less able to cope on his own. The small strokes had resulted in his left arm being considerably weaker than his right, and his inability to find the right word when speaking was cause for concern – confirmed by hospital tests which showed that Pa was suffering from a mild form of dementia. I arranged for someone to come in every day to prepare his meals, and for the district nurse to come to the cottage to give him his insulin shots. His doctor prescribed medication to help with the word finding – what we called his 'brain pills' – but the first prescription he was given gave him weird hallucinations. He told me that he would be lying in his bed at night and would see people wandering about his room. I asked him if they were unpleasant, and he replied, 'No, but I did wonder what they were doing there!' When Pa's consultant heard about this the medication was rapidly changed and, thankfully, the hallucinations stopped straightaway.

Winter came, and we were in a quandary about what to do for the first Christmas without my mother. Initially, Tony thought he would not want to be at home at the cottage but later decided that that was exactly where he wanted to be. Any married couple with parents on either side will appreciate that Christmas can be something of a diplomatic minefield as everybody needs to be visited. The problem becomes compounded when the married couple have both been married before, and there are children on both sides. However, careful negotiations were carried out, and a plan took shape where we would have a quiet Christmas Day – with myself, Ross and Ross's mother, who lived not far away – followed by a riotous Boxing Day with the rest of the family descending on the cottage. Christmas Day passed peacefully and, after Ross had returned from taking his mother home, we all went to bed. During the night I awoke to hear Pa murmuring but assumed he was talking in his sleep. Just as it was getting light, I awoke and could still hear him mumbling, so I decided to visit the bathroom and then make sure that he was all right. I didn't have to go far to find out that he wasn't. He was lying stretched out on the bathroom floor quite rigid and mumbling unintelligibly. I ran back and shook Ross awake, and between us we carried him into his bedroom and put him on his bed. I stood there, staring at him in alarm, and Ross gently touched my arm. 'I think we need the quack,' he said quietly.

There aren't many drawbacks to living in an idyllic country cottage miles from anywhere – but one of them is that the telephone is occasionally out of order due to branches of trees rubbing the wire or squirrels nibbling through it. I knew my father had the home telephone number of his doctor in his studio, so I ran out to find his phone book, then subsequently discovered that the phone was dead. Thank God for mobiles, and thank God mine still had some battery left. I rang the doctor from the end of the garden – the only place where there is a reasonable signal – and told him what had happened. 'Oh dear,' he said, 'it sounds like a major stroke. Do you want him to go to a private hospital?' I said I did and he told me he would arrange for an ambulance to come and take Pa to Guildford. Shivering, I went back upstairs to where Ross was watching over my father, who was lying quietly by this time. It wasn't long before the ambulance crunched its way over the gravel and two wonderful paramedics came in to help us. We told my father what was going on, and he opened his eyes, smiled and tried to say 'Hallo', but he couldn't form the word properly.

The men carefully carried my father downstairs and out to the ambulance; I went in the ambulance with them, and Ross followed in his car. Pa lay quietly as we made the short trip to Guildford, the paramedic every now and then laying the back of his hand on my father's cheek. All the way to the hospital the paramedic talked to me of trivial things, stopping me from thinking of the worst this might mean for my father. We arrived, and Pa was quickly whisked into a room while I wrote out a cheque for the ambulance. The doctor had told me on the phone that an NHS ambulance only delivered to NHS hospitals free of charge – a delivery to a private hospital had to be paid for. I had not wanted him to go onto a public ward where people might recognise him. If he had suffered a major stroke, I reckoned he would want to get on with it in private.

A team of nurses descended on his room, and Ross and I were politely but firmly ejected and asked to take a seat at the end of the corridor. I went out of the building to telephone everybody who was due to come for Boxing Day lunch and tell them what was going on and not to come. When I went back inside, there was to my horror the most appalling noise coming from my father's room, the bellowing and shouting was unbelievable – it seemed impossible that it was emanating from such a gently-spoken man as my Pa. Ross and I sat unhappily at the end of the corridor, tightly holding hands listening to the racket. Doors along the corridor were closing quietly, and we heard one patient say, 'What on earth is going on?' 'It's an emergency admission,' came the reply. 'Not the sort of thing we usually have in here!' said the patient. A nurse popped out and said to us, 'I am sorry about this, it must be awful for you to listen to,' and disappeared back into the room. Ross quietly put a comforting arm around my shoulders.

Suddenly, the noises stopped, and after a few moments the nurses came out smiling all over their faces. One of them came over to us and told us that my father had been furiously resisting and roaring unintelligibly while they had been undressing him and getting him plumbed into drips and catheters and everything else, but when they had put a glucose drip into his arm, he had suddenly stopped bellowing and said 'Stop it!' The team of nurses assumed they had imagined it, and carried on with what they doing, when he opened his eyes and inquired politely, 'What are you doing?'

The major stroke had turned out to be a massive diabetic hypo that had been put right by the glucose drip, and soon Ross and I were allowed in to see him. The last thing he remembered, he told us, was going into the bathroom before going to bed. He knew nothing of his uncomfortable night on the bathroom floor, or the ride in the ambulance, or of the incredible noise he had been making. The hospital wanted to keep him in for a few days to make sure his blood sugar levels were stable and told us to go home. Our traditional Boxing Day turkey curry had been made and was ready to be eaten, and it was not yet midday, so I rang everybody up again and told them to come and eat it. In the knowledge that my father was going to be fine, our lunch was positively hilarious, and many toasts were drunk to his speedy recovery. We went back to the hospital before returning to our own home in north Buckinghamshire, and found him in good spirits and perfectly comfortable. Reassured that he was in the best place possible, we drove northwards to collapse into our own beds.

My father stayed in hospital for the best part of two weeks, and I drove down every three or four days to see him. Although he felt well, his blood-sugar levels were all over the place, and his consultant did not want to let him go until they were stable.

Eventually, after two weeks, they decided that the levels were stable enough, and a date was set for me to take him home. I had arranged to stay his first night at the cottage with him, and went to the hospital to collect him. He was sitting in a chair by his bed, everything packed up and ready to go. 'Hallo, my old firework,' I said, adopting the term of endearment used by Pop Larkin in one of my father's favourite trilogies by H E Bates, 'I've come to break you out of here!' His face lit up, and we made our way out, with him stopping to thank and kiss the nurses on the way. Once back at home, I unpacked his bags. We had a drink while I prepared supper, and then watched an old film until it was time to go to bed. I tucked him up, kissed him goodnight and went to my room where I fell asleep almost instantly.

A few short hours later, I awoke to hear the same unintelligible mumbling that I had heard on Boxing night, and rushed into his room. He was on the floor. 'Oh Pa,' I said, heaving him up into a sitting position, 'this will not do.' 'No it won't!' he replied. With my help, he got to his feet, and back into bed. Trembling, I went back to mine where I lay rigid, listening for the slightest sound. Within what seemed like moments, I heard a crash and a scream. I flew into his room and found him once again on the floor, and this time he had hit his head on the radiator on the way down. I tried to sit him up, but he was making no sense at all, so I put a pillow under his head and a cover over him. For the second time in three weeks I found myself ringing the doctor's home early in the morning. This time, although he was on his way to visit another emergency patient, he came to the house. He came upstairs and looked at my father.

'Hallo Tony,' he said. 'What have you been up to?' My father replied with an unintelligible babble. 'Hmm,' said the doctor turning to me, 'He's not making a great deal of sense, is he?' Quickly he took a blood-sugar reading, and once again it was very low. He gave him an injection, and then between us we got my father back onto his bed. 'I've got to go,' he said, 'but he'll be all right in a few minutes. Call me if you have any more problems.' By the time he had put his medical equipment into his bag and was halfway out of the room, my father was beginning to return to normal.

'Who was that?' he asked me.

'Graham,' I replied.

'Graham? Graham?' said my father, looking quite astonished.

'Yes, Graham!' floated the doctor's voice drily from the bottom of the stairs. 'Good gracious,' said my father, 'what was he doing here?' It is amazing how quickly a diabetic returns to normal after a severe hypo once the sugar levels have been restored. By that afternoon, we were shopping in the local town, and it seemed that my father was perfectly fine.

The nurses continued to visit to administer the insulin injections, and each day a care assistant went in for a couple of hours to cook and look after him. For about a week, everything seemed fine. Then one day, he was out shopping with one of the care assistants who had been late in arriving to drive him into town. The result was that by the time they were on their way home it was way after lunchtime; his blood-sugar levels plummeted and once again he was in the throes of a hypo, with lips drawn back and heels drumming. The care assistant immediately stopped the car and by an enormous stroke of luck, the vehicle immediately behind was being driven by a nurse. She stopped, and very quickly an ambulance was called; my poor Pa found himself once again back in hospital. It was another week before everyone was happy with his blood-sugar levels, but it was painfully apparent that he could no longer manage with carers visiting on a daily basis.

So began the regime that continued for the rest of my father's life. A series of full-time live-in carers arrived. The first was extremely competent, saw that he was well dressed and well fed – but she wasn't a bundle of fun. Then came another to cover temporarily; she laughed a lot and delighted him by wearing in the evening while they were watching television just a T-shirt that was decent by about an inch. Her full-time replacement arrived a short while later and life suddenly became fun again for my father. Marlie was a kind and gentle girl from South Africa. Not only did she make sure he was well groomed and well fed, but they enjoyed each other's company, and she was as much friend as carer. Under this loving care, Pa bloomed, so much so that we put into action a plan I had been hatching for some while.

His studio was full of artworks, and at a time when my father was not well at all and I had cause to wonder how much longer he would be around, I had decided that these should be auctioned off to raise money for his favourite charities. But as he was so well, it seemed a much better idea to make an event of it in which he could take part and enjoy. Because of his time in India as a young man, a charity very dear to my father's heart was the Gurkha Welfare Trust. This organisation was established in 1969 as an independent charity for the relief of poverty-stricken Gurkhas of the British Crown and their dependants. In Nepal, where these men come from, there is no state welfare, and at the time of writing, the Welfare Pension provided by the Trust is the only income received by more than 10,000 veterans who do not qualify for an army pension, and all of this income is provided by fund-raising. So we carefully picked ten artworks, hired the Tithe Barn at Loseley Park and booked the Band of the Brigade of Gurkhas. We printed a catalogue of the artworks, and produced bidding paddles featuring a pair of crossed kukris (curved Gurkha knives) on one side and, with the permission of David Sproxton and Peter Lord, a cheery image of Morph on the other.

Oh what a learning curve it was! When mounting an event of this kind, it is unwise to rely on press and publicity to put bums on seats. It is, however, extremely wise to contact every friend, relative and colleague you have to tell them what is going on. We had loads of publicity, local radio and local press. Loseley Park provided sparkling wine and a fabulous curry lunch and the Band of the Brigade of Gurkhas put on a wonderful display, with the musicians marching and the dancers whirling and leaping with their kukris flashing in the sunlight under the majestic cedar trees that adorn the lawn in front of the stately home. But only 40 people came.

Ross and I got to the park early to set up the pictures on easels so that they could be viewed before the auction. The Gurkha Welfare Trust had arranged for two Queen's Gurkha Officers in full dress uniform to come and be a Gurkha presence during the event. While we masked our worry at the number of people we knew were due to turn up and prayed for a late surge, the QGOs arrived and

226

asked me what I would like them to do. I certainly didn't want them handing round canapés, and for a moment was at a loss as what to suggest – but then with a flash of inspiration, I asked if they could provide an escort for my father, taking him to his seat at lunch, and guiding him whenever he moved around. So when Tony and Marlie arrived shortly afterwards, my father, to his total delight, found himself immediately flanked on either side by these two charming and gorgeously uniformed Gurkha officers.

Everyone enjoyed the band except me – I was busy leaping around trying to recruit some more guests for lunch from visitors to the gardens who stopped to watch, with some small success. The wine sparkled and the curry lunch was delicious, but Ross and I couldn't enjoy it properly. My father, on the other hand, was having a wonderful time talking with his old friends Ray Alan, Colin Bennett, Clive Doig and Christopher Pilkington – and always with Marlie and a QGO at his elbow.

We had booked a charity auctioneer, a flamboyant character in the shape of John 'Fingers' Fingleton. Over lunch, I asked him morosely how he thought the auction might go. 'You never can tell,' he said, 'Sometimes the small events are the best.' The plates were cleared away, and Ray Alan gave a short speech in praise of my father, then introduced Fingers. Trying not to think of the bill for Loseley Park, or the cost of the hire of the band, Ross and I held our breaths as the first picture, a small coloured painting of Packi, the little white elephant, was carried up by the QGOs and displayed to our small audience. Fingers started the bidding at £100. Quickly it rose through £150, £200, £250, £300 – and sold for £350. Ross and I looked at each other wordlessly. The next picture, a detailed cartoon of jungle animals, also started at £100 – and reached £700. Suddenly Ross and I relaxed – it was going to be all right. All the pictures went, averaging £500 each – and to my delight, one of them was bought by the couple who had been watching the band and whom I had press-ganged into coming in for lunch.

The band took themselves away, having declined to join us for the curry lunch as they were having curry at their barracks on their return, and having had already consumed a vast plate of sandwiches. The guests talked to each other for a while and gradually drifted off – ten of them clutching a Tony Hart original under their arms. And one of the great things about knowing everybody who came is that I know exactly where each of those artworks are housed. Marlie took my father home, while Ross and I dismantled the easels. Completely wrung out but delighted with the way the day had turned out, Ross and I took ourselves home, vowing that if we ever did this again, we would not charge so high a ticket price for a lunchtime event, we would not chase so much publicity, but we would contact every single person we knew well in advance and tell them to bring their friends. When we finally got home neither of us felt like cooking, so we telephoned for a takeaway. Curry.

Although the symptoms of dementia were gradually becoming more pronounced, Pa's good physical health continued and, in October 2006 at his request, we decided to mount a trip to his beloved Italy. With Ross in tow, and a crash-course in administering medicines and the insulin jabs, we felt the two of us could provide Pa with sufficient care for a week's visit. Bags were packed, a sturdy walking stick was employed and away we went, taking with us a small supply of Glucogel – a high concentrate of glucose to be administered in the event of a hypo.

The journey went smoothly, and the abandon with which Pa threw aside his stick in order to embrace his friend Guglielmo at Le Agavi was a joy to behold. For the next few days we spent our time walking and eating and drinking, and my father even attempted a swim in the hotel pool – however, this was bad idea, and it took one of the hotel staff pulling Pa from above and me pushing inelegantly from below to get him out of the water. After that, he was content to relax on a sunbed in the soft, warm air and drink in the peerless view along the Mediterranean coast, the sparkling sea strewn with its litter of boats of all different shapes and sizes – cruise ships pausing to gaze at the shore, fishing boats plying their nets, boats taking tourists to the islands of Capri or Ischia, and tiny rowing boats meandering aimlessly but joyfully among them.

Having not lived with Pa on a daily basis, I wasn't aware that more exercise than usual would have a significant effect on his blood sugar. A gentle walk in the sunshine of more than a mile back down the hill from Costantino's restaurant after lunch one afternoon provoked the onset of a spectacular hypo in the hotel restaurant that evening. One moment my father was contemplating the menu and considering soup by way of a starter, and the next he was lying back in his chair with his lips drawn back and his heels drumming on the marble-tiled floor. Stupidly, I had not brought my handbag with his Glucogel in it, and Ross went flying back to our room to get it while I leaned over Pa trying to talk him back into the here and now – horribly aware of the other diners looking around curiously to see what was going on. Very quickly Pa came to his senses, and Ross arrived back at the table clutching my handbag with its precious Glucogel, only to find us having a perfectly sensible conversation about our food, which had arrived. But not for long. A few minutes later the heel drumming started again and I immediately squirted half the contents of the Glucogel tube down his throat. Its magical properties took instant effect, and after a short pause my father finished his soup with a little bread and decided that an early bed would be a good idea. We took him to his room where I helped him into his pyjamas and tucked him into bed, but he was complaining of a stomachache.

'Is it really bad?' I asked him. 'Well it's not very good,' he replied. We decided that a visit from the local English-speaking doctor was called for, and duly arrived, swathed in a gentle fragrance emitting notes of garlic and tobacco. Now it seems to me that in England if we are unwell we are prescribed pills; in France, suppositories; and in Italy, it's an injection. The doctor prodded Pa's tummy and announced that he was all blocked up and immediately prepared a hypodermic syringe. Administering the injection, the Italian doctor told my father that he would be better in the morning and to go to sleep now. We saw the doctor out, and after tucking my father in once more, I kissed him goodnight. Ross and I went to our room and collapsed into bed, leaving the door ajar in case we were needed during the night. Within what seemed like moments of our turning out the light, I heard anguished moans coming from the room next door; I leapt out of bed and ran down the corridor and into Pa's room to see what was going on. The doctor's jab for dealing with Pa's tummy had been spectacularly effective, and my poor darling dad had raced for the loo but not quite made it. Suffice to say, an instant cleanup operation was mounted. I whizzed Pa into the bathroom and showered him down, while the night manager at Ross's request sent a man with a mop and a bucket to deal with the floor. Eventually, we had the room restored to rights, and Pa clad in a fresh pair of pyjamas in his bed and sleeping like a baby. Wearing the white hotel dressing gowns, Ross and I sat at the foot of Pa's bed like a pair of fallen guardian angels and watched over him for an hour until we decided it was safe to leave him and tiptoe out of his room to collapse into our own bed once more.

The following morning, I walked along the tiled corridor to Pa's room and found him up and washed, and ready to be helped to dress. I put a short-sleeved shirt on him first, and then pulled his pyjama bottoms down from underneath it, 'To preserve your dignity,' I told him. I looked up to find him regarding me with an expression of such twinkling amusement that I could only voice what he was so obviously thinking –'…what little there is left of it!' Falling about with laughter, and loving him for the endearing way in which he accepted his increasing limitations with humour and without protest, I completed his dressing and we went down to breakfast.

The rest of the holiday passed without incident, although it has to be said that for somebody who is not quite steady on his feet, Positano with its hundreds of steps is perhaps not the ideal place to be – in actual fact Pa said of it himself that you can walk up or down but hardly ever sideways. But with a strong arm under Pa's elbow, taking each step at a time and building up a rhythm to the muttered mantra of 'step together, step together' we could achieve the 50-metre descent to the pool, or the shorter walk up the statue of the Madonna who gazes serenely out over the bay, without mishap.

We made a trip to the spectacular ancient town of Pompeii, which was really a bit too much for him – although he did delight in looking at some of the mosaics. But rather than travelling about the Neopolitan Riviera, he was happiest staying in the hotel and spending the preprandial hour each evening sipping a drink on one or other of our balconies, watching one of the world's most beautiful coastlines disappear into a smudge of indigo as darkness fell. At the end of the week, we arranged to meet up with the Capraros at a restaurant down on the waterfront, but although the hotel bus could take us down into the centre of the town, there are no public roads that go right down to the shore, and Pa certainly wasn't able to walk all the way down the steps.

But in Positano, with the help of Guglielmo, everything is possible. We got off the bus at its normal stop and then walked a few short steps to the spot where the porters who carry goods down to the restaurants on the waterside on little flatbed trucks made their base. Our bus driver accompanied us and commandeered one of the larger flat-bed trucks and its driver. We pressed my father tenderly into the front seat while my husband and I jumped into the back and, sitting on sacks on the floor of the truck leaning our backs against the cab, we gazed up at the stars as we were driven down the service road which skirts the town and winds its way past the rubbish skips, the police station and the sewage works, all the way down to the beach. There we found the Capraros, boisterous and belligerent as ever and, although they were deeply saddened not to have my mother there with us, they were utterly delighted that we had brought their old friend to see them again, and we spent our last evening in Positano in their noisy and cheerful company.

On the journey home, the beginnings of another hypo on the plane were swiftly averted. Halfway through the week, we found to our dismay that we had used up our supply of Glucogel, but a foray down to the farmacia (chemist) resulted in the purchase of glucose and a baby's drinking cup to hold in readiness in the event of another attack. There was an interesting moment at the airport after we had checked in and were going through security, when we found the security staff regarding our glucose with some mistrust. Explaining that it was neither cocaine nor a plastic explosive, and that it could prove disastrous not to have it with us on the plane, Ross and I enthusiastically tasted it to prove it was innocuous and were eventually allowed to take it on board. An hour into the flight, with lunch having been served, I noticed Pa with enormous concentration carefully dipping a piece of his bread roll into an empty wine glass. Recognising this as the onset of a hypo, we broke out the drinking cup and glucose, and the employment of these under the watchful eye of a helpful BA steward, quickly had him flying level once more.

A car was waiting for us at Gatwick to take us home. When we got home Ross and I handed my father over to the infinitely more professional care of Marlie, who was waiting on the doorstep to receive her charge as we pulled into the driveway.

It was a source of irritation that some time later an article appeared in one of the national tabloids which dwelt upon my father's disabilities, appearing to suggest he was able to take little joy in anything and describing the fact that he was no longer able to draw as 'the greatest cross he had to bear'. Yes, life had become difficult for my Pa, but one of his most endearing qualities was that if there were any crosses to bear he bore them uncomplainingly. Indeed with regard to his care, I always made a point of asking if everything was all right, and then would have to read him like a book to detect if there was anything amiss and drag it out of him. Perhaps he did not want to upset me with anything adverse – which purely illustrates his uncomplaining nature.

Interestingly, in this same newspaper there was coverage of the Turner Prize Exhibition at the Tate gallery, which for that year included a work featuring a naked shop window dummy sitting on a lavatory. There was also mention of, and pictures from, a piece of video art showing a person vomiting onto a stone floor. Possibly the artist was making a statement, or had some deep message to deliver, but it was not in my mind apparent in either of these artworks. Certainly this kind of art draws attention by its shock value – but, as Ross succinctly observed, where is the joy? Where is the joy in either the execution or the beholding of such a piece of work. And what is its inspiration to others? I remember discussing this type of art with my father some years before. Talking about Tracey Emin's work of the dirty bed variety he said, 'I don't know why she goes in for this outrageous kind of stuff – she's actually rather good.' But of course he appreciated how the hype of something deliberately designed to shock could quickly catapult an artist into the public eye. It is something he never attempted to do, and I have to confess to taking no little satisfaction in learning that the naked shop window dummy sitting on its lavatory did not win the Turner Prize.

The only time my father could have been accused of producing a piece of artwork that was shocking came about through necessity being the mother of invention – and was never shown. For an item on one of his *Vision On* programmes, he wanted to make a mobile out of inflated balloons, inside each of which would be a cut-out character drawn on cardboard that would revolve inside the balloon on a piece of thread. But to actually insert one of his cut-outs through the narrow neck of a standard balloon meant that the character had to be so small that its detail was lost. So he searched for a wide-necked balloon without success until he hit upon the perfect thing – a condom. It worked perfectly. He could put a good-sized cutout through the neck of each one and blow it up, creating a splendid bouncing, bobbing mobile of gently revolving characters. He showed it to his producer, Patrick Dowling, who was impressed with what he had achieved.

'How did you get those characters into the balloons?' he asked. 'They're not balloons,' replied Pa. Patrick studied the mobile carefully for some moments, and then realisation dawned. 'No!' he exclaimed. 'Absolutely not. This is a children's programme for goodness' sake!'

By the spring of 2007 Marlie had gone, but a bevy of delightful girls continued to take care of my father, some of them also very special to him like Sigi and Estelle from South Africa, Louise from Sweden, Sarah from Devon and Maree from Australia. As he became frailer, it became necessary for him to have two carers, one for day and one for night. But despite this, he still went off to do the occasional gig with Roc. He wasn't able to draw or make a speech any more, but it didn't matter. All he needed to do was smile and say hello, and the people came and thanked him for all the generations he had inspired, entertained and encouraged to have a go at making pictures. And on warm and sunny days, we held the shadows at bay and sat in his beautiful Surrey garden and drank wine and laughed.

EPILOGUE

The two years that followed our trip to Italy in 2006 established a routine punctuated by milestones that revealed the gradual decline in my father's health. Each May, we attended the annual reunion lunch of the 1st Gurkha Rifles in Winchester. Each June or July, we would attend one of the cricket fixtures at Wormsley. Each December, Ross and I took him to Westminster Abbey for the Children of Courage awards ceremony, and at Christmas he would come and stay with us. As time went by, his speech became harder to understand, and he found it more and more difficult to find the words that he wanted to say. His left arm was almost useless and there was little strength in his right arm and hand. Chest infection after chest infection sent him back to hospital time and time again, but despite this, he remained cheerful, and was constantly asking if we could make a return trip to his beloved Italy. With his health in such a poor state, we knew that this was just not possible.

Unbelievably, but with Roc's help, my father was still making personal appearances. Although he could not make a speech or sign autographs, people still wanted him to just be present at their launch or opening – and it did him so much good. His carers at this time were a brother-and-sister team, Maree and Leigh from Australia, who did their best to keep my father as independent as possible and always made sure that he was impeccably turned out to meet his public. In May 2008, Ross and I took him to Winchester for the reunion lunch, but although he was delighted to see many of his old friends, he could not converse with them; and while he dealt with his salmon pâté on toast with his fingers, he couldn't manage a spoon or fork, and so I fed his main course to him – an exercise to which he submitted with his usual good humour. He was able that day, however, to deal with his wineglass – he could pick it up, sip from it, and only needed a bit of help in steering it back down on the table. That brought a sparkle to his eyes.

But still the chest infections continued – and this was due mainly to Pa's increasing inability to swallow properly, which was causing him to choke. In August his consultant made a suggestion – they proposed to put in a PEG – a tube that would go directly into his stomach and through which he would be fed. 'It's a trade-off,' the consultant told me. 'If we don't do this, he won't be around for very long, but if we do, and he still enjoys seeing friends and family, going out for walks and trips, he will still have some quality of life.' So the consultant, the carers and I discussed this with Pa at great length to make sure he understood and agreed with what was planned. His consultant bluntly asked, 'You don't want to die just yet, do you Tony?' 'No!' replied my father emphatically, and he duly went down to the operating theatre to undergo the procedure. It went well, and he was returned to his hospital room in due course with a tube that attached him to a bag of feed – a mixture of vitamins and minerals and everything his body needed. But my heart ached for him, knowing how much he had always enjoyed his food and drink – a brandy and soda or a glass of wine; curry with dhal or rare roast beef; scrambled eggs; spare ribs; goat. Almost all of the happy gatherings he had enjoyed throughout the years had been centred around eating and drinking, and now it had to stop. As his consultant said, it was a trade-off – no more swallowing of food and drink in return for less likelihood of choking or infection. He could still have the pleasure of seeing family and friends gathered around the table, but he wouldn't be able to take part in the sharing of food and wine. But he appreciated the humour of what his consultant proposed. 'Tony,' he said, 'you can still sniff the wine and we can put a little on your tongue for you to taste – and if you like we'll put the rest through the tube so you still get the effect!'

It was the little tastes that gave Pa the most pleasure, and kept him as part of any social occasion where people were eating and drinking. However, these drops on a teaspoon had to be kept to a minimum, as even these tiny tastes could go down the wrong way. Maree and Leigh took up the challenge of keeping Pa stimulated by completely removing the focus of food. Suddenly he found himself in a whirl of concert-going, trips to the cinema and theatre, attending exhibitions. As he thoroughly enjoyed being driven about, Maree and Leigh would often drive him up to see us rather than my going down to see him every week. The rest of us, of course, had to eat and so we developed an informal picnicky style of eating, keeping the main focus on each other rather than the food. Although speaking was difficult, on occasion Pa would manage to reply to a question with a single, pithy word. Taking my father for a gentle stroll down the garden to see our chickens, Ross remarked on all the events Pa was attending and asked if he enjoyed them. 'Sometimes,' replied Pa with a smile.

One side effect of the PEG that we hadn't anticipated was that with the strict regulation of the feed that was being pumped into Pa, his sugar levels remained steady and the hypos became a thing of the past. He could walk reasonably well on the flat and his health was generally good. In view of all this, I approached his consultant and asked if another trip to Italy would be possible. Obviously either Maree or Leigh would have to come too, since administering my father's medication was by this time a complicated business and neither Ross nor I were trained for it. 'How long would you go for?' asked his consultant. 'Three or four days,' I replied. 'I think you can,' he said. 'I think it will be good for him.'

So in October 2008 the reservations were made. Guglielmo was ecstatic at the prospect of seeing Pa again, and we each packed a small suitcase and took one big one for all the medicines, tubes, disposable gloves, syringes and bags of feed. These we had to carry with us on the plane, as even the remotest chance of losing the bag of medicines would have been disastrous. Happily, the doctor's letters whisked us through the business of checking in without a problem. Before we left, my father was in a fever of excitement. 'How – how long ...?' the words failed him, but I knew he was asking how long we were going for. 'Three days,' I told him. He looked at me appalled. 'Just three days?' he said. I explained all the various reasons for the shortness of the trip – Pa's health, Ross's and my availability, cost. 'But just three days!' he said sorrowfully. 'But they will be three wonderful days!' I told him. And, to a degree, they were, although on that first night at Le Agavi as we were getting Pa ready for bed, he suddenly announced, 'I want to go home!'

This change of heart had been another reason for the briefness of our visit, which, with the stress of the journey and the change in his routine, I had anticipated. However, we quickly established a new routine. Ross and I became assistant shower nurses to Maree, and each morning we took it in turns to help get Pa showered, shaved and dressed. Then we went down to the restaurant; happily, although it was October, it was still warm enough to sit outside on the terrace, so Pa could look at the wonderful view while the three of us quickly ate our breakfast. On the first morning, Guglielmo came out of his office to greet my father and held Pa's hands in his while Pa just beamed and beamed – but he could not speak.

We did all the things that my father had always done: we went up to Costantino's – a worry because there were 14 steps up from the road into the restaurant and we thought we would have to carry him in a chair, but Pa had said he thought he might be able to manage it – and, motivated by the prospect of seeing his old friends again, he did. We went down to the hotel's private beach and, sitting in the shade, we read to him from one of his favourite books – H E Bates's *A Breath of French Air*. We met the Capraros for another noisy, happy evening, although they were saddened to see the deterioration in my father. We went for a drive along the stunning Amalfi coast and in the evenings we sat on one or other of our balconies and I read the manuscript of this book to him. On our last night, when I was perched at the end of his bed while Maree was busily syringing tubes and changing bags, he suddenly said, as clear as a bell, 'Darling' (which is something he hadn't called me for a long time) and then, with some difficulty, 'Thank you for the … the … words.' With a glow in my heart, I tucked him up and wished him goodnight in my usual way, saying, 'Goodnight, my old firework!' which, as always, provoked a chuckle of merriment.

We came home. October soon melted into November and all too soon Christmas had come round again, and Pa was becoming more and more frail. We went to Westminster Abbey as always, but this time he was more comfortable being pushed in a wheelchair – although once inside the Abbey he insisted on walking to his seat. He enjoyed the choir and hummed along with the carols but mostly slept through the rest of the ceremony. As always, however, in Poet's Corner afterwards, he revelled in seeing all the faces, both old and new, who came to greet him and to thank him for the years of entertainment, his talent and his inspiration.

Christmas Day arrived, and with a party that included my husband and I, four grown-up children, two ex-spouses, one mother, one grandchild, one father and two carers, an informal picnic-style lunch would not do. So I laid the table with care, setting at my father's place a Christmas cracker and, for him to look at, a photograph I had recently found of a large group of friends and family at a dinner dance taken in the seventies. During the meal, he had a taste or two of wine but was somehow apart from the rest of us, keeping up a constant singing, which would sometimes fall to a low hum, or rise to what was almost a scream. After lunch, we repaired to the sitting room for the traditional ceremony of opening Christmas presents, where, with wrapping paper littered all over the floor, my stepson Alec decided to barricade himself behind the sofa and hurl fast and furious missiles made from screwed-up wrapping paper at all and sundry. Within seconds, a blizzard of similar missiles was being chucked back at him amid shrieks of laughter, and, on being handed this ammunition Pa joined in and was throwing his paper missiles with gusto.

Almost immediately after Christmas, Maree went back to Australia for a holiday – Leigh had already gone – and two new girls were taking care of my father as I slipped back into the weekly visiting routine. Then, one weekend early in January, one of the girls rang to say that there was a flood in the studio. Ross and I tore down to find that a water pipe had frozen and burst and was gushing merrily over the floor, which was now some four inches under water. We turned the water off and set about baling out the studio. It didn't take too long, and happily there wasn't much artwork resting on the floor – although I did perform the comedy routine where a cardboard box full of stuff that has been sitting in water is picked up, and the bottom falls out and the contents spill out all over the floor. So we cleared that up too and then went into the house to see Pa.

He was delighted to see both of us, quite sparkly and not in the least concerned about the flood in the studio. He was sitting in his chair watching one of his favourite films – *The Wind Cannot Read*, a story about a young British officer who falls in love with an oriental girl who dies of a brain tumour. I went to sit beside Pa and took his hand. He turned to me and said, 'Going to die soon. Very sad.' I assumed he meant the girl in the film and agreed that it was. We stayed for a cup of tea and then took ourselves back home.

The next day, Pa was coughing badly, so the girls called my father's doctor to the house as they feared he had developed another chest infection. The doctor telephoned me to confirm that this was the case, and he was admitting him once again to Mount Alvernia Hospital. I drove down to Guildford every other day to see him, and as always, he was treated with the greatest care, dignity and kindness, but this time he didn't come home. My darling dad died in the early hours of Sunday morning, on the eighteenth of January 2009, aged 83, and it seemed to me that with his passing, the world was a poorer place.

When someone gets married, there is often more than a year to arrange the wedding. When someone dies, you've got a week to arrange the funeral. But arrange it we did, and while I knew Pa would not want anything outrageous, I felt it should be something a little out of the ordinary. It was Pa himself who told me when I was quite young that when someone dies, it is the spirit that goes, and you are left with 'a bit of old shell that needs to be disposed of with all rite and ritual.' But it was important to me that the rite and ritual should be carried out properly.

One of the first things to happen was that I was contacted by one of the Queen's Gurkha Officers who had been present at our fund-raising event, offering himself in full dress uniform as a Gurkha presence and another soldier as a piper – both of which I accepted instantly. We chose the hymns and decided that four people would speak on the various aspects of my dad, then we needed to find a piece of music for reflection. One useful thing about Pa being so well known was that once the BBC had been told and had broadcast the news, we hardly needed to call and tell anybody as they had already heard and were busy ringing us with their condolences. But I was still not entirely happy with our proposed funeral service and felt it needed something else. Driving my son to college two days after Pa died, and feeling utterly wretched and miserable, I suddenly had an idea that cheered me up enormously. At the entrance of the church we would have a large, plain canvas with paints and brushes, and pens and markers, ready to hand. As everyone arrived, they would be invited to make a mark, thus creating a bright combined work of art, which seemed to me a fitting tribute. And that's exactly what we did.

The speakers were myself, sharing memories on Tony the father; my Uncle Michael who spoke about Tony the brother; Pa's friend and producer Christopher Pilkington talking about Tony the TV artist; and Will finishing up with a reflective piece studded with sparkling wit on Tony the man. The choice of music for quiet reflection was obvious. Like warm hands softly squeezing our shoulders as the sunlight shone through the church windows, George Martin's *Elizabeth & Essex* soothed and calmed us, and we began to feel whole again.

After the church service, only the immediate family went to Guildford Crematorium to say the final farewell – with one last poignant piece of music: *Serenade for Strings* by Pa's old choirmaster, William Lloyd Webber. Back at the house, we found more than 100 people had managed to cram themselves into the cottage and, in Pa's studio, lovingly placed on the central table where he did all his work, the huge, bright, colourful and truly terrible artwork that everybody had helped to create at the church. Squiggles, spots, lines, cartoons, a pair of crossed kukris from the Gurkha Rifles, signatures and hand-prints in red, blue, yellow, green and black. Everyone had gleefully had a go – doing exactly what Pa had spent a lifetime encouraging people to do.

In the days that followed the funeral, I made the discovery that I wasn't an only child after all. No, no revelations! Simply the realisation that my father had been truly loved by thousands and thousands of people, who also wanted to pay tribute to the man with whom they had grown up and for whom they had rushed home from school to watch on television. On social networks, in books of remembrance on websites, by letter, by phone, the messages of sadness and support from people I had never met were overwhelming and enormously comforting.

One of these, Ruth Steadman, posted on Facebook the suggestion that on Sunday, 1 March 2009, as a tribute to my father, people should make a model of Morph and bring it to London's South Bank outside the Tate Modern as an impromptu 'flashmob'. Soon an events page was set up, and hundreds of people were adding their names saying that they would be there. Deciding that all these people were completely potty, and wondering whether four, forty or four hundred people would turn up, Ross and I made our way down to London to see what was going on. And thank goodness we did! We arrived outside the Tate Modern to find some two hundred models of Morph on parade, looking like some kind of psychedelic cartoon Terracotta Army. Red Morphs, blue Morphs, grey Morphs, orange Morphs, Morphs in hats, Morphs in bikinis, squished Morphs – even one young chap dressed in an orange hoodie with Morph eyes attached to the hood who went to stand quietly among the six-inch high models. All these wonderful people had travelled to the South Bank – some from as far away as Brighton and Ipswich – to come and offer their own personal tribute. We had telephoned Will on the way down to let him know what was happening, and by chance, he was already in London and said he would make his way to the South Bank.

TONY HART – A PORTRAIT OF MY DAD

So my present and previous husbands watched in some amazement as reporters from the papers, radio and television, realising that there was an appealing story in this event, grabbed me for interview after interview. One of the reporters, having finished his questioning and released me for the next one, went over to Ross and Will to check what my surname was as there was some confusion. (My married surname is, of course, Ross, but having been a Williams for more than 20 years I still use that name, managing to confuse myself and everybody else.) Ross turned to Will and said 'I don't know – whose wife is she today?' The enterprising journalist later wrote me up as 'Tony Hart's daughter, Carolyn'.

The event page in Facebook had announced that there would be a competition for the best Morph. This I duly judged, and picked a beauty of a winner – almost as good as an Aardman Morph – with his arms outspread and holding a pink flower in one hand. And all the while this was going on, I was holding another model of Morph made by Ruth Steadman that had been handed to me by a friend of hers. Tragically, Ruth had been unable to come herself as her own father, who had been very ill with cancer, had died the previous day. One of the reporters for BBC News 24 asked me if I had made the Morph I was holding, and so I was able to explain live on air that not only had Ruth made the Morph, but also that the whole 'Morphmob' tribute to my father had been her idea, and how at the last minute she had been unable to attend herself having just lost her own father. Ruth later told me how her family, watching the television at home in the midst of their grief, erupted into cheers of delight as the army of Morphs, including her own, appeared on the screen.

I met Ruth some months later at the Hazlitt Arts Centre in Maidstone at the unveiling of a commemorative plaque to Pa and we talked about losing our fathers. After her father had been diagnosed with terminal cancer, he and she were walking together and he told her that after he'd gone he would 'send her a postcard'. Now, many months after losing my father, I find I am still receiving 'postcards' – little things you come across that give you pause and make you smile. The first postcard I received was very shortly after Pa had died. I was beginning to clear things out of his studio and had just embarked on sorting a vast box of photographs. I was, I have to say, feeling totally wretched, and had just pulled myself more or less together after a little weep when I came across a Polaroid photograph of my mother, obviously taken by my father. She was clad in un-alluring but sensible underwear, apparently engaged in some kind of inelegant Pilates-style of exercise. It made me laugh out loud. Then there were the sunsets. During the week between Pa's death and his funeral, there was a succession of sunsets so unbelievably beautiful that they took my breath away. As more than one person wrote in his book of remembrance, he must have indeed been inspiring the angels to create artwork in the sky.

But his greatest legacy are those very people that he inspired and who continue to create and go on to inspire others. The best part of the Morphmob day was at the end, when all the film crews and reporters had gone and people were beginning to drift away, and about five or six people were quietly waiting to speak to me and wanting to tell me that their careers – in graphic design, in portraiture, in teaching art, in animation – had been inspired by my dad. I can think of no greater tribute, other than to add that this charming, funny, knowledgeable and hugely talented gentle man always was, and always will be, my hero.

So long my old firework. See you next time.

POSTSCRIPT

YEARS AGO I DREW A
SILLY LITTLE BIRD
THAT MY WIFE LIKED —
SHE KEPT IT
BECAUSE IT MADE
HER SMILE . . . . .

JEAN HART
1930 - 2003
TONY HART
1925 - 2009

When someone has been cremated, there remains the question of what to do with the ashes. Some people like to keep their loved one close by in an urn on the mantelpiece. Some have them scattered in the crematorium rose garden. Some people like to have them interred in a familiar churchyard, while others scatter or inter the ashes in a place or places where their loved ones were most happy. I opted for these last two. Bearing in mind Pa's dictum that any earthly remains are just a bit of old shell that needs to be disposed of with all rite and ritual, it is that very rite and ritual that brings such comfort to those who are left behind.

Pa and I had interred my mother's ashes in the garden of the cottage six years before, and now, with my daughter's help, we removed some of these and added some of Pa's to those already there. Hattie took some of the mixed ashes away with her in a flowerpot stuffed with primroses and forget-me-nots from the garden, and I took some home with me to share a pot with a beautiful pink rose that my mother had given me for my birthday a year or two before she died. A very small amount of the mixed ashes went into a little jewellery box, and the bulk of the remainder went to the funeral parlour.

The little jewellery box was important, because shortly after Pa died, I was determined that there would be another trip to Italy in order to show Hattie and Alistair the place that their grandparents had loved so much. Guglielmo had already received the sad news, but was delighted when I contacted him again to ask if they had rooms for Ross and myself, and for Tony and Jean's *nipoti* – their grandchildren. Of course they did, and so off we went in the middle of May. Hattie and Alistair were stunned by the beauty of the coastline around the Bay of Naples, enchanted by the exquisite Le Agavi hotel, and revelled in the incomparable Italian food. All the wonderful people at the hotel were sad for our loss, but had seen how very frail Pa had become on our previous visit, and understood how life had not held the same enjoyment for him then as it had in previous years. But they were very happy indeed to see the *nipoti*.

My little jewellery box of ashes sat in the bottom of my handbag. One afternoon, after Hattie and I had walked slowly up the road that winds its way from Positano after lunch in the town, and while Ross and Ali took the harder route via the steps, we approached the statue of the Madonna that stands high above Positano looking down over the town and the bay. My father had loved this statue and most evenings after dinner, he and my mother, and later he and Ross and I, would take the short walk to this shrine and spend a while gazing along the coast ablaze with the lights of the towns and villages. So on this warm May afternoon, Hattie and I spent a moment looking at the Madonna, and then at the view over the Mediterranean – brilliant blue in the afternoon sunlight. Then we tipped the little box, allowing the ashes to cascade with the barest whisper of a sound as they fell through the leaves down over the side of the mountain by the Madonna, content that a tiny part of my mother and father would remain in the place that they loved so much.

Of course we saw the Capraros, and took one of their wonderful boat trips to the island of Capri, sailing through the Faraglioni

Rocks, visiting the grottos and stopping to swim in the azure sea – and hopefully igniting in the *nipoti* the same passion for this neck of the Italian woods shared by my parents and myself.

My mother and father had lived for more than 40 years in Shamley Green, and due to their friendship with Cuthbert, along with weddings and christenings, not to mention his own frequent attendance on a Sunday in later years, my father had strong links with Christ Church. So it seemed only right that the remainder of their ashes should be interred in the churchyard. A simple stone was ordered, initially just with my parents' names and dates, but then I thought that there ought to be something else on the stone – something to denote Pa's artistry. For some years during his early career, he had always added a small snail to any drawing of his, and I thought that perhaps this snail would be appropriate to add to the stone. But then I stumbled across a piece of paper in his studio. It was a cartoon drawing of a bird, and a message – 'Years ago I drew a silly little bird that my wife liked – she kept it because it made her smile …' So we scrapped the snail and sent the little bird for the stonemason to engrave on their memorial tablet.

As is the way of these things, a perfect date presented itself – 2 September 2009, which would have been my parents' 56th wedding anniversary. Just a tiny group of us gathered in the churchyard of Christ Church on that date – Will, Ross, Hattie and me. Bob Heyes, who had conducted Pa's funeral service, also took charge of this last piece of rite and ritual. The sun shone and a soft, warm wind played about us as we stood in the grassy churchyard, breathing in the sweet smell of the yew trees. Bob read the prayers and then passed his bible to Hattie, asking her to read Psalm 139, which she did beautifully. After the Lord's Prayer, Will and I lowered the little casket into the ground, and then each of us put a trowel-ful of earth on top of it. 'Shall we fill it in now?' asked Bob. Ross stepped forward – 'I'd like to do that, if that's all right?' he said. Of course it was, and he set to with a will, taking spade-fuls of earth from the wheelbarrow that had been left close by. Suddenly Ross's spade went through the bottom of the wheelbarrow and earth poured through its disintegrated bottom onto the ground below. With enormous presence of mind, Ross simply pushed the rest of the earth through the gaping hole in the bottom of the barrow, and then continued to shovel from the pile he had created. We all roared with laughter while Ross finished the job, and felt very certain that there were two others close by, laughing too.

Lastly, I knelt down to place the stone tablet on top, adjusting it to make sure it was sitting squarely. Then I got up and we all stood back and looked at the names of my parents inscribed on the clean, white stone, and the comic little bird.

The last bit of rite and ritual was complete, and there remained nothing more to do but go and have lunch, drink wine, and talk and remember and laugh.